Perfecting Your Pronunciation: A Comprehensive Guide for Everyone

Antonio

TABLE OF CONTENTS

Chapter 1: Introduction to Pronunciation 08

Importance of Pronunciation

Benefits of Improving Pronunciation

Common Pronunciation Challenges

Overview of the Book

Chapter 2: Understanding Sounds and Articulation 16

Introduction to Phonetics

Vowels and Consonants

Voiced and Voiceless Sounds

Articulation Points

Chapter 3: Stress and Rhythm in Speech 24

Understanding Word Stress

Sentence Stress and Intonation

Mastering Syllable Stress

Developing Natural Rhythm

Chapter 4: Vowel Sounds   32

Long and Short Vowels

Diphthongs

Pronouncing Unfamiliar Vowel Sounds

Practicing Vowel Sounds

Chapter 5: Consonant Sounds   40

Plosive Consonants

Fricative Consonants

Nasal Consonants

Approximant Consonants

Pronouncing Difficult Consonant Sounds

Exercises for Consonant Sounds

Chapter 6: Word and Sentence Stress   54

Recognizing Stressed and Unstressed Syllables

Placing Stress in Multisyllabic Words

Stress in Compound Words

Stress in Sentence Patterns

Prachticing Word and Sentence Stress

Chapter 7: Intonation and Pitch 74

Understanding Intonation Patterns

Rising and Falling Intonation

Asking Questions with Intonation

Expressing Emotions Through Pitch

Developing Intonation Skills

Chapter 8: Common Pronunciation Mistakes 94

Mispronunciations of Vowel Sounds

Mispronunciations of Consonant Sounds

Common Stress and Rhythm Errors

Overcoming Pronunciation Challenges

Chapter 9: Strategies for Improvement 110

Listening to Native Speakers

Mimicking Native Pronunciation

Recording and Analyzing Your Speech

Seeking Feedback and Guidance

Incorporating Pronunciation in Daily Life

Chapter 10: Accent Reduction Techniques
130

Understanding Accents and Dialects

Techniques for Accent Reduction

Embracing Your Unique Voice

Achieving Clarity in Speech

Chapter 11: Building Fluency and Confidence
146

Practicing Pronunciation Regularly

Speaking with Native English Speakers

Engaging in Conversations and Discussions

Overcoming Fear and Shyness

Celebrating Progress and Success

Chapter 12: Resources for Continued Learning 167

Online Pronunciation Tools and Apps

Pronunciation Courses and Workshops

Pronunciation Communities and Forums

Recommended Books and Literature

Creating a Personalized Learning Plan

Chapter 13: Conclusion 187

Recap of Key Concepts

Reflecting on Your Pronunciation Journey

Embracing Lifelong Learning

Final Words of Encouragement

Chapter 1: Introduction to Pronunciation

Importance of Pronunciation

In the world of language education, pronunciation holds a crucial role in effective communication. Whether you are a beginner or an advanced learner, perfecting your pronunciation is essential for conveying your ideas clearly and ensuring that you are understood by others. In this subchapter, we will delve into the significance of pronunciation and explore the reasons why it deserves your attention.

First and foremost, pronunciation plays a vital role in enhancing your overall language skills. It is not merely about sounding like a native speaker; it goes beyond that. Correct pronunciation allows you to effectively communicate your thoughts, ideas, and emotions to others, enabling you to establish meaningful connections and build strong relationships. It ensures that your message is delivered accurately, preventing any misinterpretations or misunderstandings.

Moreover, pronunciation is closely tied to listening skills. By improving your pronunciation, you will also enhance your ability to understand spoken language more accurately. When you become proficient in identifying the subtle nuances of pronunciation, you will find it easier to comprehend different accents, dialects, and speech patterns. This, in turn, will boost your confidence when engaging in conversations with native speakers and broaden your cultural horizons.

Furthermore, mastering pronunciation can significantly contribute to your professional growth. In today's globalized world, businesses seek employees with excellent communication skills. Correct pronunciation reflects your attention to detail, professionalism, and dedication to effective communication. It can create opportunities for career advancement, as it demonstrates your ability to interact confidently and fluently with colleagues, clients, and partners.

Lastly, pronunciation is an essential component of language fluency. Fluency is not just about speaking quickly or using complex vocabulary; it also involves clear and accurate pronunciation. When your pronunciation is correct, you can focus on the content of your speech rather than struggling to articulate words. This frees your mind to think more creatively, allowing you to express yourself more naturally and fluently.

In conclusion, the importance of pronunciation in language education cannot be overstated. It enhances overall language skills, improves listening abilities, contributes to professional growth, and fosters language fluency. By dedicating time and effort to perfecting your pronunciation, you will unlock a world of opportunities and become a more confident and effective communicator in any language.

Benefits of Improving Pronunciation

In today's globalized world, language education has become increasingly important. Whether you are a student, a professional, or a traveler, having strong pronunciation skills can greatly enhance your communication abilities and open doors to various opportunities. This subchapter will delve into the numerous benefits of improving pronunciation, highlighting how it can positively impact individuals in the field of language education.

Firstly, mastering proper pronunciation allows individuals to be easily understood by native speakers. Clear and accurate pronunciation ensures that your message is conveyed effectively, eliminating any potential misunderstandings. This is particularly crucial for language learners, as mispronunciations can often lead to confusion or even embarrassment. By investing time and effort into improving pronunciation, learners can boost their confidence and fluency, enabling them to engage in meaningful conversations and build connections with native speakers.

Furthermore, improving pronunciation enhances listening skills. Language education is a two-way process, and being able to understand native speakers is just as important as being understood. By refining pronunciation, learners become more attuned to different sounds and intonations, enabling them to decipher spoken language more efficiently. This not only facilitates comprehension but also allows learners to pick up nuances and idiomatic expressions, ultimately improving their overall language proficiency.

Moreover, accurate pronunciation has a direct impact on one's speaking abilities. When learners are able to articulate words clearly and accurately, they are more likely to be perceived as fluent and credible speakers. This can be particularly advantageous in professional settings, where the ability to communicate effectively can make or break career opportunities. Employers often value individuals who possess strong verbal communication skills, and mastering pronunciation can contribute to an individual's professional growth and success.

Lastly, improving pronunciation fosters cultural understanding and appreciation. Language is deeply intertwined with culture, and by honing pronunciation skills, individuals gain insight into the cultural intricacies associated with a language. They learn to appreciate the nuances of different accents and dialects, thereby fostering cross-cultural connections and a deeper understanding of diverse societies.

In conclusion, the benefits of improving pronunciation are far-reaching. From enhancing communication and listening skills to boosting professional prospects and fostering cultural appreciation, refining pronunciation can greatly impact individuals in the field of language education. By investing time and effort in perfecting pronunciation, learners can unlock a world of opportunities and become more confident and effective communicators.

Common Pronunciation Challenges

In the world of language education, mastering pronunciation can be a daunting task. Whether you are a native speaker looking to improve your communication skills or a non-native speaker striving for fluency, there are common challenges that individuals face when it comes to pronunciation. This subchapter aims to shed light on these challenges and provide valuable insights for everyone seeking to perfect their pronunciation skills.

One of the most prevalent issues is the mispronunciation of sounds unique to a particular language. For example, English has numerous vowel and consonant sounds that may not exist in other languages. The challenge lies in training the mouth, tongue, and vocal cords to produce these sounds accurately. This subchapter will delve into specific techniques and exercises to overcome this hurdle.

Another common challenge is the incorrect stress placement within words and sentences. Stress is a vital aspect of pronunciation as it helps convey meaning and can significantly impact the clarity of your speech. This subchapter will explore different stress patterns in various languages and provide strategies to improve stress placement, ensuring effective communication.

Many individuals struggle with intonation, which refers to the rise and fall of pitch in speech. The incorrect use of intonation can make your speech sound monotonous or convey unintended meanings. This subchapter will address the importance of intonation and guide readers on how to use it appropriately to enhance their overall pronunciation.

Furthermore, the influence of one's native language on pronunciation is a significant challenge for non-native speakers. Certain sounds or sound combinations may be absent or differ in their native language, making it difficult to produce them accurately. This subchapter will offer specific exercises and techniques tailored to different language backgrounds, helping readers overcome this obstacle.

Lastly, the subchapter will touch upon common pronunciation challenges related to word and sentence stress, linking sounds within words, and the rhythm of speech. By understanding these challenges and practicing targeted exercises, readers will be able to improve their pronunciation and enhance their overall language skills.

In conclusion, this subchapter aims to provide a comprehensive guide for everyone seeking to perfect their pronunciation skills. By addressing common challenges in language education, readers will gain valuable insights, techniques, and exercises to overcome pronunciation obstacles. Whether you are a native speaker or a non-native speaker, this subchapter will guide you towards achieving clear and effective communication.

Overview of the Book

"Perfecting Your Pronunciation: A Comprehensive Guide for Everyone" is an essential resource for anyone looking to improve their pronunciation skills in any language. This book is specifically designed to cater to individuals from all walks of life, regardless of their language background or proficiency level. Whether you are a language enthusiast, a student, a professional, or simply someone looking to enhance your communication skills, this book is here to help you perfect your pronunciation.

The book begins with an introduction that emphasizes the importance of pronunciation in effective communication. It highlights how clear and accurate pronunciation can significantly impact your ability to be understood and build strong connections with others. Understanding this, the book aims to provide readers with a comprehensive guide that covers the fundamental aspects of pronunciation.

The chapters in this book are structured to take you on a step-by-step journey, starting with the basics and gradually progressing towards more advanced techniques. Each chapter delves into a specific aspect of pronunciation, such as vowel sounds, consonants, stress patterns, intonation, and rhythm. The content is presented in a clear and concise manner, making it easy to follow and implement.

What sets this book apart is its interactive approach. Throughout the chapters, you will find practical exercises, audio samples, and pronunciation drills to help you practice and reinforce what you have learned. These exercises are designed to be engaging and enjoyable, allowing you to actively participate in your learning journey.

In addition to the core content, the book also includes valuable tips and strategies for overcoming common pronunciation challenges. It addresses specific issues that learners from different language backgrounds may encounter and offers guidance on how to overcome them effectively.

"Perfecting Your Pronunciation: A Comprehensive Guide for Everyone" is a versatile resource that can be used for self-study, classroom instruction, or as a reference guide. It is written in a user-friendly manner that ensures accessibility to learners of all levels. Whether you are a beginner or an advanced learner, this book will provide you with the tools and knowledge to enhance your pronunciation skills and communicate with clarity and confidence.

In conclusion, "Perfecting Your Pronunciation: A Comprehensive Guide for Everyone" is an indispensable companion for anyone seeking to improve their pronunciation skills. With its comprehensive content, interactive approach, and practical exercises, this book will empower you to take your pronunciation to the next level. Start your journey towards clearer and more effective communication today.

Chapter 2: Understanding Sounds and Articulation

Introduction to Phonetics

In today's interconnected world, language skills have become increasingly important. Whether you are a student, a professional, or someone who simply loves to communicate, having a good command of pronunciation can make a significant difference in how effectively you convey your thoughts and ideas. Welcome to "Perfecting Your Pronunciation: A Comprehensive Guide for Everyone," a book designed to help you master the art of pronunciation.

The subchapter you are about to explore, titled "Introduction to Phonetics," serves as the foundation for your journey towards perfecting your pronunciation skills. Phonetics is the study of the sounds of human speech, and understanding its principles will give you the tools to improve your pronunciation in any language.

In this subchapter, we will delve into the basics of phonetics, exploring the various speech sounds and their production. We will introduce you to the International Phonetic Alphabet (IPA), a powerful tool used by linguists and language educators worldwide. With the IPA, you will be able to accurately represent and reproduce the sounds of any language, enabling you to enhance your pronunciation skills.

Furthermore, we will examine the concept of phonemes, which are the smallest units of sound that distinguish one word from another in a language. By understanding phonemes, you will gain insight into the subtle differences that can completely change the meaning of a word.

We will guide you through exercises and examples to help you identify and produce these essential phonemes accurately.

Throughout this subchapter, we will also explore the importance of stress and intonation in speech. These elements play a crucial role in conveying meaning and emotion, and mastering them will greatly enhance your ability to communicate effectively.

"Introduction to Phonetics" is designed to be accessible to everyone, regardless of your current language proficiency or educational background. Whether you are a language learner, a teacher, or simply someone interested in improving your pronunciation skills, this subchapter will provide you with a solid foundation to build upon.

Prepare to embark on an exciting journey of discovery and improvement as we unravel the intricacies of phonetics together. By the end of this subchapter, you will have gained valuable insights and practical techniques that will empower you to perfect your pronunciation and become a more confident and effective communicator.

Are you ready to take the first step towards unleashing your linguistic potential? Let's dive into the fascinating world of phonetics and embark on this transformative journey together.

Vowels and Consonants

Understanding the distinction between vowels and consonants is essential for perfecting your pronunciation in any language. Whether you are a language enthusiast, a student, or a professional in the field of language education, this subchapter will provide you with a comprehensive guide to mastering the art of vowels and consonants.

Vowels are the building blocks of spoken language. They are produced by allowing air to flow freely through the vocal tract without any significant obstruction. In English, we have five main vowel sounds: /a/, /e/, /i/, /o/, and /u/. These sounds serve as the foundation of many words, and being able to produce them accurately is crucial for effective communication.

Consonants, on the other hand, involve some degree of obstruction in the vocal tract. They are formed by either partially or completely blocking the airflow. English has a wide range of consonant sounds, such as /p/, /b/, /t/, /d/, /k/, /g/, /s/, /z/, /f/, /v/, and many more. Each consonant sound requires a specific placement of the articulators (e.g., lips, tongue, teeth, etc.) to produce it correctly.

To perfect your pronunciation, it is vital to pay attention to both vowels and consonants. Practice the correct placement of your articulators to produce accurate sounds. Pay attention to the duration, pitch, and stress patterns associated with each sound. Additionally, be mindful of the differences between voiced and voiceless consonants, as well as the distinction between long and short vowel sounds.

In this subchapter, you will find detailed explanations and step-by-step exercises to help you develop a clear understanding of vowels and consonants. You will also learn about the International Phonetic Alphabet (IPA), a powerful tool for representing and transcribing sounds from any language. By familiarizing yourself with IPA symbols, you will be able to accurately identify and reproduce the sounds of various languages.

Perfecting your pronunciation is a journey that requires time, dedication, and practice. By mastering the art of vowels and consonants, you will significantly enhance your ability to communicate effectively in any language. So, let's delve into the fascinating world of vowels and consonants and embark on this exciting linguistic adventure together.

Voiced and Voiceless Sounds

In the world of language education, mastering pronunciation is a key aspect for effective communication. One fundamental concept to understand is the distinction between voiced and voiceless sounds. These two categories play a crucial role in shaping the sounds we produce when speaking.

Voiced sounds are created by vibrating the vocal cords. When producing a voiced sound, such as the /z/ sound in the word "zebra," the vocal cords come together and vibrate, resulting in a resonant and audible sound. Other examples of voiced sounds include /b/, /d/, /g/, and /v/. These sounds are produced by engaging the vocal cords and allowing air to pass through, creating a distinctive tone.

On the other hand, voiceless sounds are produced without vibration of the vocal cords. These sounds are created solely by manipulating the airflow through the vocal tract. The /s/ sound in the word "snake" is an example of a voiceless sound. Other common voiceless sounds include /p/, /t/, /k/, and /f/. These sounds are created by restricting or blocking the airflow, resulting in a sharper and more muted sound.

Understanding the distinction between voiced and voiceless sounds is crucial for individuals learning a new language. This knowledge enables learners to differentiate between similar-sounding words that may only differ in terms of voicing. For example, in English, the words "pat" and "bat" differ only in their initial sounds, /p/ being voiceless and /b/ being voiced. Mispronouncing these sounds can lead to confusion and misunderstandings.

Perfecting your pronunciation requires practice and conscious effort. By focusing on distinguishing between voiced and voiceless sounds, learners can enhance their ability to produce accurate and intelligible speech. Engaging in activities such as minimal pairs exercises, where words with only one sound difference are practiced, can be highly beneficial in reinforcing these distinctions.

Remember, mastering the distinction between voiced and voiceless sounds is not only important for learners of a foreign language but also for individuals seeking to refine their pronunciation in their native tongue. By delving into the intricacies of these two sound categories, you can truly perfect your pronunciation and enhance your overall communication skills.

Whether you are an aspiring language learner or simply someone looking to refine their speaking abilities, understanding voiced and voiceless sounds is a valuable step on your journey towards effective communication. By grasping this concept, you will unlock a world of clarity and precision in your pronunciation, enabling you to express yourself with confidence and fluency.

Articulation Points

In the realm of language education, one of the fundamental aspects of achieving perfect pronunciation is understanding and mastering articulation points. These points, also known as points of articulation, are specific areas in the mouth where sounds are produced by the movement and interaction of various speech organs. By familiarizing yourself with these crucial points and practicing their correct usage, you can greatly enhance your ability to communicate effectively in any language.

The articulation points can be classified into different categories based on the specific speech organs involved. The major categories include the lips, teeth, tongue, palate, and vocal cords. Each category plays a vital role in producing distinct sounds and phonemes.

Starting with the lips, they are responsible for creating various bilabial sounds such as "p," "b," and "m." By understanding and properly utilizing the lip articulation point, you can ensure the accurate pronunciation of these sounds.

Moving on to the teeth, they are involved in producing sounds like "th" as in "think" or "this." Proper positioning and airflow through the teeth are crucial for mastering these sounds.

Next, the tongue is a versatile speech organ that plays a significant role in articulating various sounds. It can produce sounds at different points, such as the tip of the tongue for "t" and "d," the middle of the tongue for "r" and "l," and the back of the tongue for "k" and "g."

The palate, specifically the hard and soft palate, also contributes to articulation. The soft palate is responsible for nasal sounds like "n" and "ng," while the hard palate affects sounds such as "ch" and "j."

Lastly, the vocal cords produce voiced and voiceless sounds. Proper control and coordination of the vocal cords are crucial for distinguishing sounds like "s" and "z," "f" and "v," or "p" and "b."

Understanding these articulation points and how they interact with each other is essential for perfecting your pronunciation. By practicing and focusing on each individual point, you can improve your ability to produce accurate sounds and develop a native-like accent.

In conclusion, articulation points are the foundation of precise pronunciation in any language. By delving into the intricacies of these points, you can enhance your linguistic skills and communicate effectively with others. Remember, perfecting your pronunciation is a lifelong journey, and mastering articulation points is a crucial step in that journey. So, embrace the challenge, practice diligently, and watch as your language skills flourish.

Chapter 3: Stress and Rhythm in Speech

Understanding Word Stress

Word stress is an essential aspect of pronunciation that greatly influences the clarity and comprehensibility of your spoken language. It refers to the emphasis or prominence placed on certain syllables within a word. By understanding and mastering word stress, you can significantly enhance your pronunciation skills and effectively communicate with others.

In many languages, including English, word stress plays a crucial role in conveying meaning. Placing stress on different syllables can completely change the meaning of a word. For example, consider the word "record." When the stress is placed on the first syllable (RE-cord), it refers to a document or a piece of music. However, when the stress is on the second syllable (re-CORD), it becomes a verb meaning to document or to save. This simple example demonstrates the importance of word stress in English and its impact on meaning.

Word stress patterns can vary across languages, making it essential to understand the specific stress rules of the language you are learning. In English, word stress generally falls on one syllable, typically a vowel, and is often louder, longer, and higher in pitch compared to other syllables. However, exceptions and irregularities exist, making it necessary to familiarize yourself with common stress patterns.

To identify word stress in English, it is crucial to pay attention to the syllables and their relative importance within a word. Stressed syllables are typically pronounced with more force and clarity, while unstressed syllables may be reduced or even omitted. By focusing on stress patterns, you can improve your pronunciation and make your speech more natural and easily understood.

Mastering word stress requires practice and exposure to spoken language. Listening to native speakers and imitating their stress patterns can help develop your own pronunciation skills. Additionally, studying stress patterns in word lists, sentences, and dialogue can contribute to your understanding and application of word stress in real-life situations.

By understanding word stress, you will be better equipped to communicate effectively in English or any other language. It will not only enhance your pronunciation but also improve your listening skills, as you will be able to identify stressed words and their importance in a sentence. So, take the time to study and practice word stress, and you will see significant progress in your language learning journey.

Perfecting Your Pronunciation: A Comprehensive Guide for Everyone is a valuable resource that delves deeper into the topic of word stress, providing practical exercises, examples, and strategies to help you perfect your pronunciation skills. Whether you are a language learner, an educator, or simply someone passionate about language education, this book will serve as an indispensable tool in your quest for effective communication.

Sentence Stress and Intonation

In the vast world of language education, there are many important aspects to consider when perfecting your pronunciation. One crucial element that often goes overlooked is sentence stress and intonation. These two components play a vital role in conveying meaning and emotion in spoken language, making it essential for everyone to understand and master.

Sentence stress refers to the emphasis placed on certain words or syllables within a sentence. By placing stress on specific words, we can highlight important information and convey the intended message more effectively. For example, in the sentence "I didn't say he stole my money," the stress on each word can change the meaning entirely. Emphasizing "I" suggests that someone else said it, emphasizing "didn't" suggests that it was implied, and so on. Understanding sentence stress is crucial in avoiding miscommunication and ensuring clarity in your speech.

Intonation, on the other hand, refers to the rise and fall of pitch in a sentence. It is the melody of speech that adds emotion and nuance to our words. By using appropriate intonation patterns, we can convey different attitudes such as excitement, surprise, or sadness. For instance, a rising intonation at the end of a sentence indicates a question, while a falling intonation suggests a statement or a command. Mastering intonation is essential for effective communication as it helps to convey the intended mood and intention behind our words.

To perfect your sentence stress and intonation, it is crucial to pay attention to native speakers and mimic their patterns. Listening to authentic conversations, audio materials, or even podcasts can provide valuable exposure to different sentence stress and intonation patterns. Practicing with a language exchange partner or a tutor can also be beneficial as they can provide feedback and correct any mistakes you may make.

Additionally, there are various exercises and drills you can incorporate into your language learning routine. Tongue twisters, for instance, can help you practice stress patterns and improve your pronunciation. Reading aloud, recording yourself, and listening back to identify areas of improvement can also be helpful in perfecting your sentence stress and intonation.

In conclusion, sentence stress and intonation are crucial aspects of pronunciation that should not be overlooked. By understanding and mastering these components, you can enhance your communication skills and express yourself more effectively. Through practice, exposure to native speakers, and incorporating exercises into your language learning routine, you can perfect your sentence stress and intonation, ultimately improving your overall pronunciation.

Mastering Syllable Stress

In the journey of perfecting your pronunciation, one crucial aspect that cannot be overlooked is syllable stress. The way we stress certain syllables in words can greatly impact our overall fluency and clarity. Whether you are a native English speaker looking to refine your pronunciation or a non-native speaker aiming to improve your language skills, mastering syllable stress is an essential step towards achieving your goal.

Syllable stress refers to the emphasis we place on certain syllables within a word. It plays a vital role in conveying meaning and ensuring effective communication. Correctly stressing syllables can help you sound more natural and confident in your speech, as well as enhance your listening skills when interacting with others.

This subchapter will guide you through the principles of syllable stress, providing you with the necessary tools to understand and apply it in your spoken language. It will cover topics such as:

1. Introduction to Syllable Stress: Learn the basics of syllable stress, including its importance and how it affects word meaning and sentence rhythm.

2. Rules and Patterns: Explore the various rules and patterns governing syllable stress in English. Understand the difference between primary and secondary stress and how to identify stressed and unstressed syllables.

3. Practice Exercises: Engage in practical exercises designed to help you recognize and reproduce syllable stress accurately. These exercises

will provide you with hands-on experience in applying the rules and patterns learned.

4. Common Challenges: Identify common challenges and pitfalls when it comes to syllable stress. Discover strategies to overcome these challenges and improve your pronunciation.

5. Listening Activities: Enhance your listening skills through targeted listening activities. Train your ear to recognize syllable stress in authentic spoken English to further develop your understanding and fluency.

Whether you are an English language learner or a language educator, mastering syllable stress is crucial for effective communication. This subchapter will equip you with the necessary knowledge and skills to confidently navigate the complexities of syllable stress and improve your overall pronunciation. By mastering syllable stress, you will unlock a new level of fluency and clarity, enabling you to communicate with confidence in any language setting.

Developing Natural Rhythm

In the journey towards perfecting your pronunciation, one crucial aspect that often gets overlooked is developing natural rhythm. Rhythm plays a vital role in language education, as it helps to convey meaning, emotion, and intention in speech. Whether you are a beginner or an advanced learner, understanding and incorporating natural rhythm into your pronunciation can significantly enhance your communication skills.

The concept of natural rhythm refers to the patterns of stressed and unstressed syllables in spoken language. Every language has its own unique rhythm, and mastering this aspect can help you sound more fluent and native-like. Just as music has a beat, language has its own beat, and by aligning yourself with this rhythm, you can improve your overall pronunciation.

One effective technique for developing natural rhythm is through listening and imitating native speakers. By actively engaging with authentic audio materials such as podcasts, songs, or movies, you can train your ear to recognize the natural flow and stresses of words. Pay close attention to how native speakers emphasize certain syllables and how they connect words together in a sentence. Mimicking their rhythm and intonation will help you internalize the patterns and incorporate them into your own speech.

Another useful strategy is to practice rhythmic patterns and drills. Start by tapping out the beats of familiar phrases or sentences, emphasizing the stressed syllables. Gradually increase the complexity, incorporating different sentence structures and word combinations.

This practice will help you develop a sense of rhythm and improve your ability to stress syllables naturally.

In addition to listening and drilling, being aware of word stress is crucial. Many languages have stress patterns that can drastically change the meaning of a word. By understanding and correctly applying word stress, you can ensure that your message is clear and accurate. Consult pronunciation dictionaries or language learning resources to familiarize yourself with the stress patterns of your target language.

Developing natural rhythm takes time and practice, but the rewards are worth it. By incorporating rhythm into your pronunciation, you will notice a significant improvement in your overall fluency. Your speech will flow more smoothly, and you will be better equipped to convey the intended meaning and emotion behind your words.

Remember, mastering pronunciation is not just about individual sounds; it is about understanding and incorporating the natural rhythm of a language. By actively engaging with authentic materials, practicing rhythmic patterns, and being aware of word stress, you can develop a natural rhythm that will greatly enhance your communication skills. So, embrace the beat of the language and perfect your pronunciation!

Chapter 4: Vowel Sounds

Long and Short Vowels

Vowels play a crucial role in pronunciation, and understanding the difference between long and short vowels is essential in perfecting your language skills. In this subchapter, we will delve into the fascinating world of long and short vowels, exploring their significance and providing you with practical tips to enhance your pronunciation.

Long vowels are pronounced with an extended sound, while short vowels have a shorter, crisper sound. The length of a vowel sound can alter the meaning of a word, so it is vital to master the nuances between long and short vowels to communicate effectively.

One of the most common ways to differentiate between long and short vowels is through duration. When producing a long vowel sound, the vocal cords vibrate for a longer period. For example, compare the short "a" sound in the word "cat" with the long "a" sound in the word "cake." The elongated sound in "cake" changes the word's meaning, emphasizing the importance of mastering long vowels.

Furthermore, understanding the distinction between long and short vowels can aid in word recognition, spelling, and comprehension. Being able to identify and produce the correct vowel sound can prevent misunderstandings and enhance your overall language skills.

To perfect your pronunciation of long and short vowels, it is crucial to practice regularly. Start by familiarizing yourself with the phonetic symbols used to represent these sounds. Additionally, listen to native speakers and imitate their pronunciation. Pay attention to the length of their vowel sounds and try to replicate them accurately. Record yourself speaking and compare your pronunciation to that of a native speaker to identify areas for improvement.

Furthermore, engaging in vowel exercises can be immensely beneficial. Practice saying pairs of words that differ only in their vowel sounds, such as "bit" and "beat," or "dot" and "boat." This will train your ears and help you recognize the subtle distinctions between long and short vowels.

In conclusion, understanding the difference between long and short vowels is paramount in perfecting your pronunciation skills. By familiarizing yourself with the phonetic symbols, listening to native speakers, and engaging in regular practice, you can master the art of long and short vowels, enhancing your overall language education. So, let's embark on this fascinating journey and unlock the secrets of long and short vowels together!

Diphthongs

Diphthongs: Mastering the Melody of Language

In the vast world of language education, one crucial aspect that often goes overlooked is the pronunciation of diphthongs. Diphthongs are unique combinations of vowel sounds that create a melodic effect in speech. Perfecting the pronunciation of diphthongs is essential for effective communication and can significantly enhance one's language skills. In this subchapter, we will delve into the intricacies of diphthongs and provide you with comprehensive guidance to master their pronunciation.

To begin, let's understand what diphthongs are. Simply put, diphthongs are when two vowel sounds merge together to form a single sound. Unlike individual vowels, diphthongs possess a melodic quality, making them integral to the rhythm and flow of speech. Mastering diphthongs can help you sound more natural, fluent, and polished in any language.

This subchapter will take you on a journey through the various types of diphthongs found in different languages. From English to Spanish, German to Mandarin, we will explore the unique diphthongs each language offers. By understanding these distinctions, you will gain a deeper appreciation for the complexity and diversity of language.

Next, we will delve into the technical aspects of producing diphthongs accurately. We will guide you through the correct tongue and mouth positions required to create each diphthong sound. Through detailed explanations and visual aids, we aim to make the learning process seamless and enjoyable.

Furthermore, we will provide you with practical exercises and drills to strengthen your diphthong pronunciation skills. These exercises will help you develop muscle memory, enabling you to effortlessly produce the correct diphthong sounds in any context. We encourage you to practice regularly, as consistency is key to perfecting your pronunciation.

In addition to the technical aspects, we will explore the cultural significance of diphthongs. By understanding how diphthongs are used in different languages, you will gain insights into the customs, traditions, and nuances of various cultures. Language is deeply intertwined with culture, and mastering diphthongs can unlock a world of understanding and appreciation.

Whether you are a language enthusiast, a student, or a professional seeking to improve your communication skills, this subchapter on diphthongs is a valuable resource for everyone. Perfecting Your Pronunciation: A Comprehensive Guide for Everyone aims to empower learners of all backgrounds to confidently navigate the intricate world of language education. Let us embark on this journey together and unlock the harmonious melody of diphthongs!

Pronouncing Unfamiliar Vowel Sounds

In the vast world of languages, one of the most challenging aspects of pronunciation for learners is mastering unfamiliar vowel sounds. Whether you're a language enthusiast, a student, or a professional in the field of language education, this subchapter is designed to help you perfect your pronunciation skills and overcome the obstacles that come with unfamiliar vowel sounds.

Understanding and reproducing vowel sounds accurately is crucial for effective communication. Different languages have their own unique set of vowel sounds, and many learners find it difficult to differentiate them from their native language. However, with the right guidance and practice, anyone can conquer these challenges and achieve excellent pronunciation.

The first step to mastering unfamiliar vowel sounds is to familiarize yourself with the International Phonetic Alphabet (IPA). This system provides a standardized representation of sounds, including vowels, from different languages. By familiarizing yourself with the IPA symbols and their corresponding sounds, you will gain a solid foundation for tackling new vowel sounds.

Once you have a basic understanding of the IPA, it's time to delve into the specific vowel sounds you find challenging. This subchapter will provide detailed explanations and examples of various vowel sounds, breaking them down into their individual components. Through clear descriptions, diagrams, and audio samples, you will learn how to position your mouth, tongue, and lips to produce each sound accurately.

To ensure effective learning, this subchapter offers practical exercises and drills to help you internalize and reproduce unfamiliar vowel sounds. These exercises are carefully designed to target specific problem areas and strengthen your pronunciation skills. By regularly practicing these drills, you will gradually develop muscle memory and improve your ability to pronounce unfamiliar vowel sounds with ease.

Furthermore, this subchapter addresses common mistakes made by learners when pronouncing unfamiliar vowel sounds. By understanding these errors and the reasons behind them, you will be better equipped to correct your own pronunciation and overcome any difficulties you may encounter.

In conclusion, mastering unfamiliar vowel sounds is an essential aspect of developing excellent pronunciation skills. Whether you're a language enthusiast or a professional in language education, this subchapter provides a comprehensive guide to help you overcome these challenges. By familiarizing yourself with the IPA, understanding the specific vowel sounds, and practicing with targeted exercises, you will become proficient in pronouncing unfamiliar vowel sounds and enhance your overall language proficiency.

Practicing Vowel Sounds

Vowels are the building blocks of language and play a fundamental role in pronunciation. Mastering vowel sounds is essential for effective communication and can greatly improve your language skills. In this subchapter, we will explore various techniques and exercises to help you perfect your vowel pronunciation.

Understanding vowel sounds is the first step towards improving your pronunciation. Vowels can be categorized into long and short sounds, as well as tense and lax sounds. Each sound is unique and learning to differentiate between them is crucial. By practicing vowel sounds, you will be able to express yourself more clearly and confidently in any language.

One effective technique to practice vowel sounds is to listen and imitate native speakers. Find audio resources such as podcasts, songs, or videos in your target language and pay close attention to how the speakers pronounce their vowels. Mimic their intonation, stress, and pitch to develop a more natural-sounding pronunciation.

Another useful exercise is to practice vowel sounds in isolation. This involves pronouncing each vowel sound individually, holding it for a few seconds, and paying attention to the position of your mouth and tongue. Experiment with different mouth positions and tongue placements to produce accurate vowel sounds. Repeat this exercise daily to build muscle memory and improve your pronunciation.

To further enhance your vowel pronunciation, try incorporating tongue twisters into your practice routine. Tongue twisters are excellent for improving clarity and fluency. Choose tongue twisters that focus on vowel sounds and repeat them at a slow pace, gradually increasing your speed as you become more comfortable. This exercise will help you enunciate vowels correctly and develop better articulation.

Finally, recording yourself while practicing vowel sounds can be a valuable tool for self-assessment. Listen to your recordings and compare them with native speakers to identify areas for improvement. Pay attention to any inconsistencies or errors in your pronunciation and work on correcting them.

Remember, mastering vowel sounds takes time and practice. Consistency is key, so make it a habit to include vowel exercises in your language learning routine. By perfecting your vowel pronunciation, you will greatly enhance your overall language skills and become a more confident and effective communicator.

Whether you are a beginner or an advanced learner, practicing vowel sounds is essential to perfecting your pronunciation. Embrace the challenge and enjoy the journey of improving your language skills through focused vowel practice.

Chapter 5: Consonant Sounds

Plosive Consonants

In the realm of language education, one of the most crucial aspects to master is pronunciation. The ability to articulate sounds accurately not only enhances communication but also adds a touch of fluency and clarity to one's speech. Among the various elements of pronunciation, plosive consonants hold significant importance. Understanding and perfecting the pronunciation of plosive consonants can greatly improve your language skills, regardless of the language you are learning.

Plosive consonants, also known as stop consonants, are produced by briefly stopping the airflow and then releasing it with a sudden burst. This creates a distinct and crisp sound that adds depth and expression to your speech. Examples of plosive consonants include the sounds /p/, /b/, /t/, /d/, /k/, and /g/. Understanding the proper articulation of these sounds is essential for effective communication.

To pronounce plosive consonants accurately, it is crucial to focus on the placement and release of airflow. For example, to pronounce the /p/ sound, gently press your lips together, blocking the airflow, and then release it by opening your lips suddenly. The /b/ sound is produced in a similar manner, but with the addition of vocal cord vibration. By paying attention to these subtle differences, you can achieve a more authentic pronunciation.

Perfecting plosive consonants requires practice and patience. Incorporating exercises like tongue twisters and minimal pair drills can greatly enhance your ability to distinguish and produce these sounds accurately. Additionally, listening to native speakers and mimicking their pronunciation can help you fine-tune your skills.

Remember that plosive consonants vary across languages. Engaging with the specific phonetic rules of the language you are learning is essential to achieving proficiency. Languages like English, Spanish, and French have their own unique set of plosive consonants, each with its own set of rules and pronunciation patterns.

In conclusion, understanding and mastering plosive consonants is a vital part of perfecting your pronunciation skills. Whether you are learning a new language or aiming to improve your fluency, focusing on these sounds will undoubtedly enhance your communication abilities. With practice and dedication, you can bring clarity and precision to your speech, making you a more confident and effective communicator.

Fricative Consonants

Fricative consonants play a crucial role in language, and understanding their pronunciation is essential for effective communication. In this subchapter, we will delve into the world of fricative consonants, exploring their characteristics, common examples, and tips for perfecting your pronunciation.

Fricative consonants are produced by creating friction or turbulent airflow through a narrow space in the vocal tract. This results in a distinct hissing or buzzing sound. Unlike other consonant sounds, fricatives are continuous, meaning they can be prolonged as long as the speaker maintains the airflow.

One of the most well-known fricatives is the "s" sound. Try saying it out loud and notice the airflow between your tongue and the roof of your mouth. Other fricatives include "f," "v," "z," "sh," and "th," both voiced (as in "that") and voiceless (as in "think"). Each fricative is unique, and mastering their pronunciation requires practice and attention to detail.

To perfect your fricative consonant pronunciation, start by listening to native speakers carefully. Pay close attention to the position of their tongue, teeth, and lips as they produce fricatives. Observe their airflow and try to mimic their sound.

Next, practice individual fricatives by isolating them in simple words. Repeat them slowly and exaggerate the sound to ensure accuracy. For example, focus on words like "six," "fish," "she," and "zip."

To further refine your pronunciation, try contrasting fricative pairs. For instance, compare "s" and "z" by saying words like "sit" and "zit." Pay attention to the difference in voicing, airflow, and tongue placement.

Remember, mastering fricative consonants takes time and patience. Be persistent and practice regularly to develop muscle memory and improve your pronunciation skills.

In conclusion, fricative consonants are an integral component of language, and learning to pronounce them accurately is crucial for effective communication. By understanding their characteristics, practicing individual fricatives, and contrasting pairs, you can perfect your pronunciation and enhance your language skills. So, embrace the challenge, keep practicing, and soon you'll be confidently producing fricative consonants like a native speaker.

Nasal Consonants

One of the key aspects of perfecting your pronunciation is mastering the nasal consonants. Nasal consonants are a unique group of sounds that are produced by allowing air to flow through the nose while blocking the oral cavity with the articulatory organs. These sounds add richness and variety to speech, and they are found in numerous languages around the world.

Understanding and producing nasal consonants can be challenging, especially for non-native speakers. However, with practice and attention to detail, anyone can improve their pronunciation of these sounds. In this subchapter, we will dive deep into the world of nasal consonants, exploring their articulation, common mistakes, and techniques to overcome them.

The subchapter begins with a thorough introduction to the concept of nasal consonants, providing an overview of the various sounds and their characteristics. We will examine the specific articulatory organs involved in producing nasal consonants and highlight the differences between nasal and non-nasal sounds.

Next, we delve into the most common nasal consonants found in different languages, such as /m/, /n/, and /ŋ/. We will provide detailed explanations of their articulation, including tongue placement, airflow, and voicing. Additionally, we will explore the variations of nasal consonants across languages, emphasizing the importance of understanding these differences when learning a new language.

To help learners overcome common pronunciation challenges, we will dedicate a section to the most frequent errors made when producing nasal consonants. We will provide practical tips and exercises to improve nasal consonant pronunciation and address issues such as nasalization, devoicing, and assimilation.

Finally, we will conclude the subchapter with a range of exercises and activities designed to reinforce the concepts discussed. These exercises will not only enhance the understanding of nasal consonants but also improve overall pronunciation skills. Learners will have the opportunity to practice articulating nasal consonants in isolation, within words, and in various sentence contexts.

Perfecting Your Pronunciation: A Comprehensive Guide for Everyone aims to provide a comprehensive resource for language learners and educators. This subchapter on nasal consonants will equip readers with the necessary tools to master these unique sounds, enhancing their language education journey. Whether you are a beginner or an advanced learner, this subchapter will help you perfect your pronunciation and communicate more effectively in any language.

Approximant Consonants

In the realm of language education, it is crucial to focus not only on vocabulary and grammar but also on pronunciation. Perfecting Your Pronunciation: A Comprehensive Guide for Everyone aims to equip learners with the necessary tools to improve their speaking skills and sound more like native speakers. In this subchapter, we delve into the topic of approximant consonants, exploring their characteristics, common examples, and techniques to master their pronunciation.

Approximant consonants, also known as semivowels, are a unique category of speech sounds that possess qualities of both consonants and vowels. Unlike true consonants, which involve complete obstruction of airflow, approximants allow for a freer flow of air. This results in a more vowel-like sound, making them an essential aspect of achieving natural-sounding speech.

One of the most common approximant consonants is the English "w" sound. Pronounced by rounding the lips and creating a slight narrowing at the back of the throat, the "w" sound is essential in words like "water" and "window". Similarly, the "y" sound in words like "yes" and "yellow" is another example of an approximant consonant. To pronounce this sound, one must lift the tongue towards the hard palate while allowing air to flow through the sides.

Mastering approximant consonants requires practice and attention to detail. One effective technique is to listen to and mimic native speakers. Pay close attention to the shape of their mouths, the position of the tongue, and the airflow. Mimicking these aspects helps develop muscle memory, leading to improved pronunciation.

Another strategy is to engage in minimal pair exercises. Minimal pairs involve words that differ by only one sound, such as "wet" and "yet". Practicing these pairs allows learners to identify and contrast the correct pronunciation of approximant consonants, further refining their skills.

Furthermore, focusing on stress and intonation patterns is crucial when working with approximant consonants. Understanding how these sounds interact with the rhythm and melody of a language greatly enhances overall pronunciation.

In conclusion, approximant consonants play a significant role in achieving accurate and natural-sounding speech. By understanding their characteristics, practicing mimicry, engaging in minimal pair exercises, and mastering stress and intonation patterns, learners can perfect their pronunciation skills. Perfecting Your Pronunciation: A Comprehensive Guide for Everyone provides the necessary guidance and exercises to help learners effectively incorporate approximant consonants into their speech, ultimately enhancing their overall language proficiency.

Pronouncing Difficult Consonant Sounds

In the vast world of language education, one of the most common challenges faced by learners is mastering the pronunciation of difficult consonant sounds. Whether you are a native English speaker or someone learning English as a second language, this subchapter aims to provide you with comprehensive guidance on perfecting your pronunciation.

Consonant sounds play a crucial role in effective communication, as they form the building blocks of words and sentences. However, some consonant sounds can be particularly tricky, often resulting in miscommunication or misunderstanding. Fear not! With the right techniques and practice, you can overcome these challenges and achieve impeccable pronunciation.

One such difficult consonant sound is the "th" sound, which is commonly found in words like "theater" or "think." Many non-native English speakers struggle with this sound due to its absence in their native languages. To master the "th" sound, try placing your tongue gently between your teeth and exhaling air as you carefully pronounce the sound. Regular practice will help you become more comfortable with this unique sound.

Another challenging consonant sound is the "r" sound, particularly for learners whose native languages do not have a similar sound. The key to pronouncing the "r" sound correctly is to place the tip of your tongue near the roof of your mouth, creating a slight vibration as you articulate the sound. Remember, practice makes perfect, so don't be discouraged if it takes time to perfect this sound.

Additionally, the subchapter will delve into other difficult consonant sounds such as the voiced and voiceless "th" sounds, the "l" and "w" sounds, and the distinction between "v" and "w." Each sound will be explained in detail, accompanied by helpful tips and exercises to assist you in perfecting your pronunciation.

Perfecting Your Pronunciation: A Comprehensive Guide for Everyone aims to equip learners of all backgrounds with the necessary tools to enhance their communication skills. By addressing the difficulties associated with consonant sounds, this subchapter caters to the needs of language education enthusiasts, whether they are students, professionals, or individuals seeking to improve their communication abilities.

Remember, the journey to perfect pronunciation requires patience and perseverance. Embrace the challenges, practice regularly, and soon you will find yourself confidently pronouncing even the most difficult consonant sounds.

Exercises for Consonant Sounds

Consonant sounds play a crucial role in our ability to communicate clearly and effectively. They form the building blocks of words and help convey meaning in our speech. However, mastering these sounds can be challenging, especially for non-native speakers. In this subchapter, we will explore a range of exercises designed to help you perfect your pronunciation of consonant sounds.

1. Minimal Pairs: One effective exercise for improving consonant sounds involves working with minimal pairs. Minimal pairs are pairs of words that differ by only one sound, such as ship and sheep or bet and bit. Practice saying these words aloud, paying close attention to the specific consonant sound that distinguishes them. This exercise will help train your ear to differentiate between similar sounds and improve your ability to produce them accurately.

2. Tongue Twisters: Tongue twisters are fun and challenging exercises that can help you improve your pronunciation of consonant sounds. They involve repeating phrases or sentences that contain a series of similar sounds. For example, "Peter Piper picked a peck of pickled peppers" focuses on the /p/ and /k/ sounds. Repeat tongue twisters slowly and gradually increase your speed as you become more comfortable. This exercise will help you develop muscle memory and improve your articulation of consonant sounds.

3. Word Stress: Another important aspect of mastering consonant sounds is understanding word stress. Some consonants can change their pronunciation depending on whether they occur at the beginning, middle, or end of a word. For instance, the /t/ sound in

"water" is pronounced differently than in "table." Practice identifying and emphasizing the stressed syllables in different words to improve your overall pronunciation.

4. Dictation Exercises: Dictation exercises can be a valuable tool for improving your consonant sounds. Listen to audio recordings or a native speaker and write down what you hear. Focus on accurately transcribing the consonant sounds, paying attention to any details or nuances. Compare your transcription with the original text to identify areas for improvement.

Remember, mastering consonant sounds requires practice and patience. Incorporate these exercises into your language learning routine, and gradually you will notice a significant improvement in your pronunciation. By perfecting your consonant sounds, you will enhance your overall communication skills and gain confidence in expressing yourself fluently and accurately in any language.

In the journey to perfecting your pronunciation, it is crucial to focus not only on vowel sounds but also on consonant sounds. Consonants play a significant role in forming words and conveying meaning, making it essential to pay attention to their correct articulation. In this subchapter, we will explore a variety of exercises specifically designed to help you improve your consonant sounds and enhance your overall language proficiency.

1. Minimal Pairs: One effective exercise to distinguish between similar consonant sounds is practicing minimal pairs. Minimal pairs are words that differ in only one sound, such as "ship" and "sheep," or "bat"

and "pat." By comparing and contrasting these similar words, you can train your ear to identify and reproduce the correct sound.

2. Tongue Twisters: Tongue twisters are not only a fun way to challenge yourself but also a great exercise for mastering consonant sounds. They help you practice articulating difficult sounds rapidly and accurately. Try saying tongue twisters like "Peter Piper picked a peck of pickled peppers" or "She sells seashells by the seashore" to improve your proficiency in specific consonant sounds.

3. Word Stress: Learning the correct stress patterns in words is crucial for accurate pronunciation. Certain consonant sounds change their quality when they are stressed or unstressed. For instance, the "t" sound in the word "butter" is pronounced differently from the "t" sound in the word "bottle." Practice stressing and de-stressing sounds in different words to develop a clear understanding of their variations.

4. Mirror Exercises: Visual feedback can be incredibly helpful in perfecting your pronunciation. Stand in front of a mirror and observe how your mouth, lips, and tongue move when producing different consonant sounds. Pay attention to the shape of your mouth, the position of your tongue, and the movement of your lips. This visual feedback will allow you to make necessary adjustments and improve your articulation.

5. Native Speaker Recordings: Listening to native speakers is an excellent way to familiarize yourself with the correct pronunciation of consonant sounds. Utilize resources like podcasts, audio recordings, or language learning apps to immerse yourself in the natural rhythm and

intonation of the language. Mimicking native speakers will help you internalize the correct pronunciation patterns.

By incorporating these exercises into your language learning routine, you will gradually enhance your ability to articulate consonant sounds accurately. Remember to be patient and consistent in your practice, as perfect pronunciation takes time and effort. With dedicated practice, you will soon find yourself speaking with confidence and clarity, making significant strides in your language education journey.

Chapter 6: Word and Sentence Stress

Recognizing Stressed and Unstressed Syllables

In the vast landscape of language education, one crucial aspect that often goes overlooked is the recognition of stressed and unstressed syllables. Pronunciation is a fundamental element of effective communication, and mastering the art of syllable stress can greatly enhance your language skills. Whether you are a student, a professional, or simply someone looking to improve their pronunciation, understanding and identifying stressed and unstressed syllables is a key stepping stone towards perfecting your speech.

Stressed syllables refer to those that are emphasized or pronounced with more force in a word, while unstressed syllables are given less prominence and are spoken more lightly. The correct placement of stress in a word can drastically alter its meaning and intent, making it crucial to grasp this concept for effective communication. Many languages, including English, utilize stressed and unstressed syllables to convey meaning and rhythm.

Recognizing stressed and unstressed syllables is not only vital for proper pronunciation but also for better comprehension. By understanding the patterns and rules of syllable stress, you can decipher the intended meaning of words and sentences more easily. This knowledge will enable you to communicate more confidently and correctly, ensuring that your message is accurately conveyed.

In this subchapter, we will delve into the intricacies of recognizing stressed and unstressed syllables. We will explore various techniques and strategies that will help you identify the stress patterns in words and sentences. From understanding the role of vowels and consonants in determining stress to recognizing the impact of word prefixes and suffixes, we will equip you with the tools needed to demystify syllable stress.

Moreover, we will provide you with ample practice exercises and interactive examples to reinforce your learning. These exercises will allow you to apply the knowledge gained and fine-tune your skills in recognizing stressed and unstressed syllables. By immersing yourself in these activities, you will develop a keen ear for stress patterns and become more attuned to the nuances of pronunciation.

Whether you are a native English speaker seeking to polish your language skills or a non-native speaker aiming to improve your pronunciation, this subchapter is designed for everyone. Perfecting Your Pronunciation: A Comprehensive Guide for Everyone recognizes that language education is a lifelong journey, and by honing your ability to recognize stressed and unstressed syllables, you are taking a significant step towards mastering the art of pronunciation.

In the vast realm of language education, one crucial aspect that often gets overlooked is the importance of recognizing stressed and unstressed syllables. Perfecting Your Pronunciation: A Comprehensive Guide for Everyone aims to rectify this oversight by shedding light on this fundamental topic.

Understanding stressed and unstressed syllables is essential for achieving clear and effective communication in any language. Each word is composed of syllables, which are units of sound. In many languages, including English, some syllables carry more emphasis or prominence than others. These emphasized syllables are known as stressed syllables, while the less prominent ones are referred to as unstressed syllables.

Why is it so crucial to recognize stressed and unstressed syllables? The answer lies in the rhythm and melody of language. Languages have their own unique musicality, with patterns of stress and intonation that contribute to natural speech flow. By recognizing stressed and unstressed syllables, learners can reproduce the natural rhythm of a language, leading to improved fluency and intelligibility.

This subchapter delves into the intricacies of identifying stressed and unstressed syllables. It presents various techniques and exercises to help learners develop an ear for stress patterns. One such technique involves listening to native speakers and identifying which syllables they stress in different words. Additionally, learners will discover the role of stress in distinguishing between words that may appear similar but have different meanings, such as "reBEL" (noun) and "rebel" (verb).

Perfecting Your Pronunciation: A Comprehensive Guide for Everyone also explores the different factors that influence stress placement. For instance, in English, stress can be determined by the number of syllables in a word, the presence of certain vowel sounds, or the part of speech of a word. By understanding these factors, learners can predict stress patterns and enhance their overall pronunciation skills.

Throughout this subchapter, readers will find practical exercises, audio examples, and engaging activities to reinforce their understanding of stressed and unstressed syllables. By mastering this aspect of pronunciation, learners will gain confidence in their language skills and be better equipped to communicate effectively in any setting.

Whether you are a language enthusiast or a language educator, recognizing stressed and unstressed syllables is a crucial step towards perfecting your pronunciation. With Perfecting Your Pronunciation: A Comprehensive Guide for Everyone, you will embark on a journey that will unlock the rhythmic beauty of language and empower you to communicate with clarity and confidence.

Placing Stress in Multisyllabic Words

In the vast world of language education, one crucial aspect that often poses a challenge for learners is placing stress in multisyllabic words. Mastering this skill is essential for effective communication and natural-sounding pronunciation. Understanding the principles behind stress placement can significantly enhance your fluency and improve your overall language proficiency.

To begin with, it is important to recognize that stress is a fundamental element in every language. It refers to the emphasis placed on certain syllables within words, which helps to convey meaning and rhythm. In English, stress is typically marked by increased loudness, length, and pitch.

When it comes to multisyllabic words, stress is usually placed on one particular syllable, known as the stressed syllable. The other syllables are considered unstressed. The placement of stress in a word often follows specific patterns, but exceptions do exist.

One common rule to determine stress placement is the concept of word formation. Many English words follow a predictable pattern, where the stress falls on the syllable that was stressed in the original word from which it was derived. For instance, the noun 'present' has stress on the first syllable, while the verb 'present' has stress on the second syllable. Understanding these patterns can provide valuable insights into stress placement.

Another factor to consider is the part of speech. In English, nouns and adjectives tend to have stress on the first syllable, while verbs often stress the second syllable. For example, 'record' as a noun has stress on the first syllable, but as a verb, stress shifts to the second syllable. Recognizing these patterns can assist in correctly placing stress in multisyllabic words.

Additionally, it is worth noting that stress placement can also influence the meaning of words. In some cases, changing the stress within a word can alter its meaning entirely. For instance, the noun 'insult' has stress on the first syllable, while the verb 'insult' has stress on the second syllable. Being aware of these nuances is crucial for accurate pronunciation and effective communication.

Mastering the skill of placing stress in multisyllabic words takes time and practice. Regular exposure to authentic spoken English, listening to native speakers, and engaging in speaking exercises can greatly contribute to your progress. By honing this essential skill, you will gain confidence in your pronunciation and take significant strides towards perfecting your language abilities.

Understanding the correct placement of stress in multisyllabic words is crucial for perfecting your pronunciation in any language. Stress refers to the emphasis or prominence placed on a particular syllable within a word. It plays a vital role in conveying meaning and ensuring effective communication. This subchapter will delve into the intricacies of placing stress in multisyllabic words, providing you with essential guidelines to improve your language pronunciation skills.

One of the fundamental rules to remember when placing stress in multisyllabic words is that not all syllables are created equal. Some syllables are naturally more emphasized, while others are less prominent. To determine which syllable to stress, we need to analyze the word's structure and consult pronunciation dictionaries or resources specific to the language you are learning.

In many languages, stress tends to fall on the penultimate or antepenultimate syllable, but there are exceptions to this generalization. For instance, in English, the placement of stress can vary greatly, making it essential to learn stress patterns for specific words or word categories. Some common patterns include stress on the first syllable (e.g., "elephant"), the second syllable (e.g., "table"), or the final syllable (e.g., "address").

In addition to recognizing stress patterns, it is essential to understand the impact of stress on the meaning of words. Placing stress on different syllables can completely change the word's meaning. For example, in English, "present" (noun) and "present" (verb) have different stress patterns, resulting in distinct meanings. Developing an awareness of these nuances will help you avoid misunderstandings and improve your overall pronunciation.

To perfect your stress placement, practice is key. Engage in activities that focus on multisyllabic word stress, such as listening to native speakers, repeating words, and participating in pronunciation exercises. Utilize resources like pronunciation apps, online courses, or language exchange platforms to receive feedback and guidance from language experts or native speakers.

By understanding the rules and patterns of stress placement in multisyllabic words and dedicating time to practice, you will significantly enhance your pronunciation skills. Remember, mastering stress in language education is essential for effective communication and building confidence in your language abilities. So, dive into the world of multisyllabic word stress and take your pronunciation to the next level!

Stress in Compound Words

Compound words are formed when two or more words are combined together to create a new word with a different meaning. In English, compound words are commonly used and play a crucial role in our daily communication. However, stress placement in compound words can often be a challenging aspect of pronunciation for language learners.

Understanding how stress is placed in compound words is essential for perfecting your pronunciation and ensuring clear and effective communication. In this subchapter, we will explore the rules and patterns that govern stress placement in compound words, providing you with a comprehensive guide to overcome this common hurdle.

One important rule to remember is that stress in compound words generally falls on the first syllable. For example, in the compound word "blackboard," the stress is placed on the first syllable, "black." Similarly, in "sunflower," the stress falls on the first syllable, "sun." However, there are exceptions to this rule, and we will delve into those as well.

Another important aspect to consider is the type of compound word. There are three main types of compound words: noun-noun compounds, adjective-noun compounds, and verb-noun compounds. Each type has its own stress placement patterns.

In noun-noun compounds, the stress is typically placed on the first noun. For instance, in "football," the stress falls on "foot." In adjective-noun compounds, the stress is usually on the adjective. For example, in "red apple," the stress is on "red." Finally, in verb-noun compounds, the stress is generally on the verb. Take "handshake" as an example, where the stress is on "shake."

However, as mentioned earlier, there are exceptions to these patterns. Some compound words have shifting stress, where the stress moves from one syllable to another depending on the meaning or context. This can be seen in words like "record" (noun) and "record" (verb), where the stress placement changes accordingly.

Mastering stress placement in compound words requires practice and familiarity with the rules and patterns. By understanding these guidelines, you can enhance your pronunciation skills and communicate with clarity and confidence.

In conclusion, stress placement in compound words is a crucial aspect of pronunciation in English. This subchapter has provided a comprehensive guide to help you perfect your pronunciation skills and overcome the challenges associated with stress in compound words. By familiarizing yourself with the rules and patterns discussed, you will be well-equipped to communicate effectively in various contexts and build your language education expertise.

Compound words play a crucial role in language education as they allow us to express complex ideas and concepts with ease. However, mastering the pronunciation of compound words can be a challenge, especially when it comes to determining which syllable to stress. In this subchapter, we will delve into the topic of stress in compound words, providing you with valuable insights and practical tips to perfect your pronunciation.

Understanding stress patterns in compound words is essential for clear and effective communication. In English, the stress pattern of a compound word is often based on the stressed syllable of its individual components. However, there are exceptions to this rule, making it necessary to develop a strong foundation in stress patterns to avoid potential confusion.

One common pattern is the noun-noun compound, where the first syllable is usually stressed. For instance, in "blackboard" and "sunflower," the stress falls on the first syllable of each word. Likewise, in adjective-noun compounds like "hotdog" and "greenhouse," the stress typically falls on the first syllable of the adjective.

In other cases, the stress may shift to the second syllable in noun-verb compounds. For example, in "heartbeat" and "brushstroke," the stress falls on the second syllable, which is the verb component of the compound.

Additionally, compound words can have two stressed syllables, particularly in adjective-adjective compounds. Consider words like "blue-green" and "high-pitched," where both adjectives are equally stressed.

To perfect your pronunciation of compound words, it is crucial to familiarize yourself with stress patterns by listening to native speakers or utilizing pronunciation tools. By doing so, you will develop an intuitive understanding of where to place stress in various compound words.

Furthermore, practicing stress patterns in compound words through repetition and imitation can greatly enhance your pronunciation skills.

Focus on stressing the correct syllables and pay attention to the rhythm and melody of the words.

In conclusion, stress in compound words is an important aspect of language education. By understanding the underlying patterns and practicing pronunciation techniques, you can confidently communicate and express yourself in any English-speaking environment. Remember, mastering stress in compound words is a step towards perfecting your pronunciation and achieving fluency in the language.

Stress in Sentence Patterns

In the realm of language education, one crucial aspect that often gets overlooked is the importance of stress in sentence patterns. Whether you are a native English speaker looking to improve your pronunciation or a non-native speaker striving for fluency, understanding and mastering stress in sentence patterns is essential.

Stress refers to the emphasis or prominence placed on certain words or syllables within a sentence. It plays a significant role in conveying meaning and ensuring effective communication. By placing stress on the correct words or syllables, you can enhance the clarity and impact of your speech.

One fundamental rule to remember is that stress in English tends to fall on content words rather than function words. Content words, such as nouns, verbs, adjectives, and adverbs, carry the most significant meaning in a sentence. On the other hand, function words, including articles, prepositions, and pronouns, serve grammatical purposes and are generally unstressed.

Another important principle to grasp is the concept of sentence stress. Sentence stress refers to the overall pattern of stress within a sentence. Native English speakers intuitively apply sentence stress to highlight the most important words or ideas. Understanding and imitating this pattern can greatly enhance your ability to be understood and to comprehend spoken English.

It is important to note that stress can also change the meaning of a sentence. By placing stress on different words within a sentence, you can alter the intended message. For example, consider the sentence "I didn't say he stole my money." By stressing different words, such as "I," "say," "he," "stole," "my," or "money," you can convey different shades of meaning and emphasize different aspects of the sentence.

To perfect your pronunciation and stress in sentence patterns, it is crucial to practice listening to and imitating native speakers. Pay close attention to how they stress certain words or syllables and try to replicate their patterns. Additionally, make use of resources like audio recordings, pronunciation exercises, and language learning apps that specifically target stress in sentence patterns.

In conclusion, stress in sentence patterns is an integral part of achieving clear and effective communication in English. By understanding the rules and patterns of stress, and by practicing and imitating native speakers, you can perfect your pronunciation and enhance your overall language skills.

In the realm of language education, mastering pronunciation is often an elusive goal for many learners. However, perfecting your pronunciation is not just about individual sounds or words; it also involves understanding and properly utilizing stress patterns in sentences. This subchapter delves into the crucial aspect of stress in sentence patterns, providing a comprehensive guide for everyone seeking to improve their pronunciation skills.

Stress, in the context of language, refers to the emphasis placed on certain syllables or words within a sentence. The correct placement of stress is vital for effective communication, as it can drastically alter the meaning and intent of a sentence. Understanding stress patterns can help learners convey their ideas accurately and be better understood by native speakers.

One key aspect of stress in sentence patterns is the recognition of stressed and unstressed words. In English, some words are naturally stressed, while others are not. By identifying and emphasizing the stressed words, learners can effectively highlight the most important information in their speech. This subchapter provides strategies and exercises to help individuals identify stressed and unstressed words, allowing them to enhance their overall pronunciation skills.

Moreover, this subchapter explores the concept of sentence stress and its impact on meaning. Sentence stress involves placing emphasis on certain words within a sentence to convey the intended message. By understanding the rules and patterns of sentence stress, learners can effectively communicate their ideas with clarity and precision. This subchapter provides practical examples and exercises to help individuals master the art of sentence stress and improve their overall pronunciation.

Furthermore, this subchapter addresses the challenges faced by non-native speakers when it comes to stress in sentence patterns. It highlights common mistakes and provides techniques to overcome these challenges. By acknowledging and addressing these difficulties, learners can make significant progress in perfecting their pronunciation skills.

In conclusion, stress in sentence patterns is a fundamental aspect of pronunciation that every language learner should strive to master. This subchapter serves as a valuable resource for individuals seeking to improve their pronunciation skills. By understanding and effectively utilizing stress in sentence patterns, learners can enhance their overall communication abilities and confidently express themselves in the target language. Regardless of your language proficiency level, this comprehensive guide will equip you with the necessary tools to perfect your pronunciation and become a more confident and effective communicator.

Practicing Word and Sentence Stress

One of the fundamental aspects of perfecting your pronunciation is mastering word and sentence stress. The way we stress certain syllables or words within a sentence can greatly enhance our communication skills and make our speech more natural and fluent. In this subchapter, we will explore the importance of word and sentence stress and provide practical exercises to help you improve in this area.

Word stress refers to the emphasis placed on a particular syllable within a word. Every word has at least one stressed syllable, and correctly identifying and pronouncing these stressed syllables is crucial for clear communication. By stressing the right syllables, you can convey meaning more effectively and avoid misunderstandings. In this section, we will delve into the rules and patterns of word stress in English, providing you with the necessary tools to identify and stress syllables correctly.

Sentence stress, on the other hand, involves placing emphasis on certain words within a sentence to convey the intended meaning. By stressing the most important words, you can guide your listener's understanding and highlight crucial information. In this subchapter, we will explore the principles of sentence stress and provide practical exercises to help you develop your skills in this area.

To effectively practice word and sentence stress, we will provide a range of interactive exercises and activities. These exercises will help you differentiate between stressed and unstressed syllables, identify the correct placement of word stress in multisyllabic words, and practice sentence stress in various contexts. By engaging in these activities, you will gradually internalize the rules and patterns, allowing you to apply them effortlessly in your everyday speech.

Remember, mastering word and sentence stress is an essential aspect of perfecting your pronunciation. It not only enhances your communication skills but also boosts your confidence as a language learner. Whether you are a native English speaker looking to refine your pronunciation or a non-native speaker seeking to improve your language skills, this subchapter provides comprehensive guidance and practical exercises to help you perfect your word and sentence stress.

So, dive into the world of word and sentence stress and unlock the key to clear and effective communication. With practice and dedication, you will soon be speaking with confidence and fluency, making your words resonate with impact and meaning.

In the realm of language education, mastering pronunciation is an essential component of effective communication. The ability to convey ideas clearly and accurately requires not only correct pronunciation of individual sounds but also an understanding of word and sentence stress. This subchapter will delve into the significance of word and sentence stress and provide valuable techniques to perfect your pronunciation.

Word stress refers to the emphasis placed on specific syllables within a word. English is a stress-timed language, meaning that certain syllables are stressed more heavily than others, leading to a rhythmic pattern. Understanding and applying word stress correctly is crucial for conveying meaning and avoiding misunderstandings. By practicing word stress, you can enhance your fluency and make your speech sound more natural.

Sentence stress, on the other hand, refers to the emphasis placed on specific words within a sentence. This stress helps to convey the intended message and create a natural rhythm in speech. By mastering sentence stress, you can effectively highlight important information and enhance the overall clarity of your communication.

To practice word and sentence stress, a variety of techniques can be employed. One effective method is to listen to and imitate native speakers. By observing how they stress certain syllables or words, you can gain valuable insights into the natural rhythm and flow of the language. Additionally, recording your own voice and comparing it to native speakers can help identify areas for improvement.

Another technique is the use of stress drills and exercises. These exercises involve identifying and stressing the correct syllables or words in a given sentence or phrase. By practicing these drills regularly, you can train your ear to recognize the correct stress patterns and develop muscle memory for producing them.

Furthermore, incorporating stress into your daily vocabulary practice can greatly reinforce your understanding and application of word and sentence stress. By actively paying attention to stress patterns when learning new words, you can internalize the correct stress patterns more effectively.

In conclusion, mastering word and sentence stress is a vital aspect of pronunciation for individuals seeking to improve their language skills. By understanding the importance of stress, utilizing various techniques, and incorporating regular practice, anyone can perfect their pronunciation and enhance their overall communication abilities. So, let's embark on this journey to perfecting your pronunciation and experience the joy of effective and confident communication!

Chapter 7: Intonation and Pitch

Understanding Intonation Patterns

Intonation patterns play a crucial role in effective communication, regardless of the language you speak. They help convey emotions, emphasize key ideas, and add depth to your speech. In this subchapter, we will explore the significance of intonation patterns in language education and provide you with practical tips to perfect your pronunciation.

Intonation refers to the rise and fall of pitch in speech. It encompasses the melody, rhythm, and tone of your voice. By mastering intonation patterns, you will be able to express yourself more accurately and engage your listeners effectively.

In language education, understanding intonation patterns is essential for both learners and teachers. For learners, it allows them to grasp the nuances of a language and sound more natural when speaking. It helps them understand the emotions and intentions behind spoken words, making communication more authentic and meaningful. For teachers, knowledge of intonation patterns helps in designing effective pronunciation lessons and providing guidance to students.

One aspect of intonation patterns is the rise and fall of pitch at the end of a sentence. This is known as sentence-level intonation. It indicates the type of sentence (declarative, interrogative, or imperative) and can change the meaning or intention behind the words. Mastering sentence-level intonation will enable you to ask questions clearly, make statements confidently, and give commands assertively.

Another important aspect of intonation patterns is stress and emphasis within words and phrases. By placing stress on certain syllables or words, you can highlight key information and convey meaning more effectively. Understanding stress patterns will help you avoid miscommunication and improve your overall fluency.

To perfect your pronunciation and master intonation patterns, practice is key. Engage in regular listening exercises to familiarize yourself with the melody and rhythm of the language. Pay attention to native speakers, mimic their intonation, and gradually incorporate it into your own speech. Record yourself speaking and compare it to native speakers to identify areas for improvement.

Additionally, seek feedback from language teachers or native speakers to fine-tune your intonation skills. They can point out specific areas where you may need to adjust your pitch or stress to sound more natural.

Understanding and mastering intonation patterns will enhance your overall language skills and make you a more effective communicator. By incorporating these techniques into your language education journey, you will be able to express yourself with confidence, fluency, and authenticity. So, practice diligently, listen attentively, and embrace the beauty of intonation patterns in your quest for perfect pronunciation.

Intonation is an essential aspect of pronunciation that greatly impacts the meaning and clarity of our speech. It refers to the rise and fall of our voice as we speak, conveying emotions, attitudes, and grammatical information. Mastering intonation patterns is crucial for effective communication, whether you are a language learner, teacher, or simply someone looking to improve their pronunciation skills. This subchapter will provide you with a comprehensive understanding of intonation and its significance in language education.

Intonation patterns vary across languages, and even within different dialects and accents. They play a vital role in distinguishing between statements, questions, commands, and exclamations. By understanding and practicing these patterns, you can convey your intended meaning more accurately and enhance your overall communication skills.

One of the fundamental aspects of intonation is the pitch, which refers to the highness or lowness of our voice. Rising pitch usually indicates a question, while falling pitch indicates a statement. Falling-rising pitch patterns are common in commands, and high pitch with a sudden drop is often used for exclamations. Learning to recognize and produce these pitch patterns will significantly improve your spoken language abilities.

Another crucial element of intonation is stress. Stress refers to the emphasis placed on certain syllables or words in a sentence. By assigning stress to the right syllables, you can convey the intended meaning and avoid misunderstandings. Understanding the stress patterns in a language is particularly important for non-native speakers, as incorrect stress placement can alter the entire meaning of a word or sentence.

Intonation also helps convey attitudes and emotions. Rising intonation at the end of a sentence can indicate uncertainty or a request for confirmation, while falling intonation can express certainty or finality. By incorporating appropriate intonation patterns, you can add depth and nuance to your speech, making it more engaging and relatable to your listeners.

In this subchapter, we will explore various intonation patterns through practical examples, exercises, and audio resources. By practicing and familiarizing yourself with these patterns, you will become more confident in your pronunciation skills and ensure effective communication in any language.

Remember, understanding and mastering intonation patterns is a lifelong journey. Whether you are a language learner or a language teacher, this subchapter will serve as a valuable resource to perfect your pronunciation skills and enhance your overall language education experience.

Rising and Falling Intonation

Intonation is a crucial aspect of pronunciation that has a significant impact on how we communicate and convey meaning. In this subchapter, we will explore the concepts of rising and falling intonation and their role in language education.

Intonation refers to the rise and fall of pitch in speech. It helps express emotions, attitudes, and meaning beyond the words themselves. Rising and falling intonation patterns are essential for effective communication and can greatly influence the way we are perceived and understood by others.

Rising intonation involves a gradual increase in pitch towards the end of a sentence or phrase. It is commonly used in questions, indicating that the speaker is seeking information or confirmation. For example, "Are you coming to the party?" The rising intonation at the end of the sentence signals that the speaker expects a response from the listener.

On the other hand, falling intonation involves a gradual decrease in pitch towards the end of a sentence or phrase. It is often used in statements, indicating the completion of a thought or idea. For instance, "I had a great time at the party." The falling intonation at the end of the sentence conveys a sense of finality or certainty.

Understanding and mastering rising and falling intonation patterns is crucial for language learners. It helps them sound more natural and native-like. Additionally, intonation can alter the meaning of a sentence or phrase. For example, a rising intonation on a statement can turn it into a question, or a falling intonation on a question can make it sound more assertive.

In language education, instructors focus on teaching rising and falling intonation through various exercises and drills. These may include listening to and imitating native speakers, practicing dialogues with different intonation patterns, and analyzing the intonation patterns in different contexts.

By perfecting rising and falling intonation, learners can enhance their overall pronunciation skills and become more effective communicators. It enables them to convey emotions accurately, ask questions confidently, and express their ideas with clarity.

In conclusion, rising and falling intonation are fundamental aspects of pronunciation that play a crucial role in language education. Mastering these patterns allows learners to communicate effectively, convey meaning beyond words, and sound more natural in their target language.

Intonation plays a crucial role in effective communication. It helps convey meaning, express emotions, and can even influence how others perceive our message. In this subchapter, we will explore rising and falling intonation, two important aspects of intonation that are widely used in language education.

Rising intonation is often associated with questions and uncertainty. When we use rising intonation, our pitch goes up towards the end of a sentence or phrase. This upward movement signals that we are seeking confirmation, asking for information, or expressing doubt. For example, when asking a question like, "Are you coming to the party tonight?", the rising intonation at the end of the sentence indicates that we are seeking a response or confirmation from the listener.

On the other hand, falling intonation is commonly used in statements and commands. It involves a downward pitch movement towards the end of a sentence or phrase. Falling intonation is typically associated with certainty, authority, and finality. For instance, when making a statement like, "I have completed the project", the falling intonation at the end of the sentence conveys that the speaker is confident and assertive about their statement.

Understanding and correctly using rising and falling intonation is vital for effective communication. It helps convey the intended meaning of our words and prevents misinterpretation. Incorrect intonation can sometimes lead to confusion or misunderstandings, especially for non-native speakers.

In language education, mastering rising and falling intonation is crucial for developing proper pronunciation and fluency. Language learners need to be aware of the intonation patterns in their target language and practice producing them accurately. Teachers play a significant role in guiding students towards correct intonation patterns, providing ample opportunities for practice, and offering feedback to reinforce their learning.

To perfect your pronunciation, it is essential to pay attention to rising and falling intonation in the language you are learning. Practice different intonation patterns, listen to native speakers, and record your own voice to compare and improve your intonation skills.

Remember, rising and falling intonation are powerful tools that can greatly enhance your communication skills. By mastering these intonation patterns, you will be able to express yourself effectively, captivate your audience, and convey your intended meaning with clarity and confidence.

Asking Questions with Intonation

In the realm of language education, mastering pronunciation is crucial for effective communication. One aspect that often gets overlooked is the proper use of intonation when asking questions. Intonation refers to the rise and fall of pitch in spoken language and plays a vital role in conveying meaning and intent.

When asking questions, using the appropriate intonation pattern can help convey curiosity, uncertainty, or even urgency. Understanding the different intonation patterns for various question types is essential for perfecting your pronunciation and enhancing your communication skills.

Wh-questions, such as "What is your name?" or "Where are you going?" typically have a falling intonation pattern. The pitch starts high at the beginning of the question and gradually falls towards the end. This falling pattern indicates that the speaker expects an informative response and is seeking factual information.

Yes/No questions, on the other hand, require a rising intonation pattern. For instance, when asking "Did you eat lunch?" or "Are you ready?", the pitch rises towards the end of the question. This rising pattern suggests that the speaker is expecting a simple "yes" or "no" answer.

Tag questions involve adding a mini-question at the end of a statement, such as "It's a beautiful day, isn't it?" or "You like pizza, don't you?" In tag questions, the intonation falls at the end, creating a rising-falling pattern. This intonation pattern indicates that the speaker is seeking confirmation or agreement.

Intonation also plays a role in expressing emotions and attitudes when asking questions. For example, when expressing surprise, the pitch may rise sharply at the end of a question. On the other hand, when asking a question with urgency or impatience, the pitch may rise quickly and be followed by an abrupt fall.

Mastering intonation when asking questions can significantly enhance your pronunciation and overall communication skills. By understanding the different patterns and how they convey meaning, you can effectively engage in conversations, demonstrate your curiosity, and express your emotions.

In conclusion, perfecting your pronunciation involves paying attention to the nuances of intonation when asking questions. Whether you are in a language education setting or simply aiming to improve your communication skills, understanding the appropriate intonation patterns for different question types will greatly benefit your ability to express yourself clearly and effectively. So, let's dive deeper into the world of intonation and take your pronunciation to the next level!

In the realm of language education, mastering pronunciation is a crucial step towards effective communication. One aspect that often gets overlooked is the art of asking questions with proper intonation. While we may understand the words and grammar rules, the way we ask questions can greatly impact the clarity and understanding of our message. In this subchapter, we will delve into the intricacies of intonation and explore how it can enhance your questioning skills.

Intonation refers to the rise and fall of pitch in our speech. It helps convey meaning, express emotions, and distinguish between statements and questions. When it comes to asking questions, intonation plays a pivotal role in guiding the listener towards comprehension. By utilizing the appropriate intonation patterns, you can effectively communicate your curiosity and engage in meaningful conversations.

One common intonation pattern for questions is the rising intonation. This is when the pitch of our voice rises towards the end of a sentence. Rising intonation is typically used for yes/no questions, where we expect a simple affirmation or negation. For example, "Did you finish your homework?" or "Are you coming to the party?"

Another intonation pattern is the falling intonation, which is employed for information-seeking questions. When we ask for specific details or request explanations, our voice typically falls in pitch towards the end of the sentence. For instance, "What time does the meeting start?" or "Why did you choose that book?"

Beyond these basic intonation patterns, it is essential to consider the context and tone of your questions. Softening your intonation can convey politeness and respect, while emphasizing certain words can add emphasis and urgency. Understanding these nuances will help you navigate various social situations and adapt your questioning style accordingly.

In order to perfect your pronunciation and intonation, it is crucial to practice regularly. Record yourself asking questions and listen for any inconsistencies or areas of improvement. Additionally, engage in conversations with native speakers or language partners, and pay attention to their intonation patterns.

By perfecting the art of asking questions with intonation, you can elevate your language skills and become a more confident communicator. Remember, effective questioning is not just about the words you use, but also how you deliver them. Develop your intonation skills, and watch as your ability to engage in meaningful conversations flourishes.

Expressing Emotions Through Pitch

Understanding how to effectively express emotions through pitch is a crucial aspect of mastering pronunciation. Pitch refers to the highness or lowness of your voice while speaking. It plays a significant role in conveying emotions, intentions, and attitudes in any language. In this subchapter, we will explore the importance of pitch in expressing emotions and provide practical tips for perfecting your pitch for effective communication.

Emotions are an integral part of human communication. They allow us to connect on a deeper level and convey our thoughts and feelings. When it comes to speaking, the pitch of our voice can greatly enhance or diminish the emotional impact of our words. By mastering pitch, you can effectively express a wide range of emotions, from excitement and enthusiasm to sadness and anger.

In many languages, pitch variations are used to indicate different emotional states. For instance, a rising pitch may denote surprise or excitement, while a falling pitch signifies sadness or disappointment. By understanding these patterns and incorporating them into your speech, you can convey your emotions more accurately and engage your listeners on a deeper level.

To perfect your pitch, it is essential to practice active listening. Pay attention to how native speakers use pitch to express various emotions in different contexts. Observe the rise and fall of their voices and the emphasis they place on certain words or phrases. By mimicking these patterns, you can develop a more natural and expressive way of speaking.

Another valuable technique is to use pitch variations to highlight key words in a sentence. By slightly raising or lowering your pitch on important words, you can convey emphasis, urgency, or even sarcasm. This can greatly enhance the overall meaning and emotional impact of your message.

It is also important to be aware of cultural differences in pitch patterns. Different cultures may have specific pitch variations to express emotions. Being mindful of these cultural nuances can help you communicate effectively with people from diverse backgrounds.

In conclusion, mastering pitch is essential for expressing emotions accurately and effectively in any language. By understanding the role of pitch in conveying emotions and practicing active listening, you can develop a more natural and expressive way of speaking. Incorporating pitch variations to highlight key words and being aware of cultural differences will further enhance your communication skills. Remember, mastering pitch is a lifelong journey, but with practice and dedication, you can perfect your pronunciation and connect with others on a deeper emotional level.

In our quest to perfect our pronunciation and communicate effectively, one crucial aspect that often gets overlooked is the role of pitch in expressing emotions. The way we modulate our voice can greatly enhance our ability to convey various emotions, making our speech more engaging and impactful. This subchapter will delve into the importance of pitch in expressing emotions and how we can harness its power to become more effective communicators.

Pitch is the melodic quality of our voice and refers to the highness or lowness of our vocal tone. It plays a crucial role in conveying emotions such as excitement, anger, sorrow, and surprise. By consciously varying our pitch, we can add depth and nuance to our speech, making it more expressive and relatable to our audience.

For instance, when expressing excitement, our pitch tends to rise, with our voice becoming more animated and energetic. On the other hand, when conveying sadness or sorrow, our pitch tends to lower, reflecting a somber and melancholic tone. By understanding these pitch variations, we can effectively convey our emotions and connect with our listeners on a deeper level.

To express emotions through pitch, it is important to develop an awareness of our own vocal range. Experimenting with different pitches in a comfortable and controlled manner allows us to discover the full potential of our voice and its ability to convey emotions. Regular practice and vocal exercises can help expand our pitch range, making our emotional expression more versatile and authentic.

Additionally, paying attention to the pitch patterns of native speakers in the language we are learning can greatly enhance our ability to express emotions accurately. By imitating their intonation and pitch variations, we can internalize the subtle nuances that make their emotional expression so effective. Listening to native speakers through audio resources or engaging in conversations with fluent speakers can provide valuable insights into the appropriate pitch patterns for different emotions.

In conclusion, pitch is a powerful tool for expressing emotions and can greatly enhance our communication skills. By understanding the role of pitch in conveying different emotions and practicing its variations, we can become more effective and engaging communicators. Developing awareness of our own vocal range and studying the pitch patterns of native speakers will enable us to express emotions accurately and connect with our audience on a deeper level. So, let's embrace the power of pitch and perfect our pronunciation to become more expressive and impactful in our language education journey.

Developing Intonation Skills

Intonation is a crucial aspect of pronunciation that often goes overlooked in language education. It refers to the rise and fall of pitch in our voice as we speak, and it plays a vital role in conveying meaning and emotion. Whether you are a native speaker or a language learner, perfecting your intonation skills can greatly enhance your overall communication abilities.

In this subchapter, we will explore various techniques and exercises to help you develop your intonation skills. By practicing these techniques, you will gain a deeper understanding of intonation patterns and how they contribute to effective communication.

One of the first steps in developing your intonation skills is to become familiar with the different intonation patterns used in your target language. Each language has its own unique intonation patterns that convey specific meanings. By studying and imitating native speakers, you can learn to incorporate these patterns into your own speech.

Furthermore, paying attention to stress and rhythm is crucial in improving your intonation. Stress refers to the emphasis placed on certain syllables or words in a sentence, while rhythm refers to the overall pattern of stressed and unstressed syllables. By practicing stress and rhythm exercises, you can enhance your ability to convey meaning and emotion more effectively.

Another important aspect of developing intonation skills is understanding the connection between intonation and sentence structure. Intonation can change the meaning of a sentence, even if the words remain the same. By learning to use rising and falling intonation patterns at appropriate points in a sentence, you can enhance clarity and expressiveness in your speech.

Furthermore, incorporating intonation into your everyday practice is crucial. Engaging in conversations with native speakers or language exchange partners is an excellent way to refine your intonation skills. Additionally, listening to podcasts, audiobooks, or music in your target language can expose you to a variety of intonation patterns and help you internalize them.

In conclusion, developing intonation skills is essential for anyone looking to perfect their pronunciation. By understanding the various intonation patterns, practicing stress and rhythm, and incorporating intonation into daily practice, you can greatly enhance your communication abilities. Remember, intonation is not just about sounding natural but also about conveying meaning and emotion effectively. So, let's embark on this journey together and perfect our intonation skills!

In the fascinating journey of perfecting your pronunciation, one crucial aspect that often gets overlooked is intonation. Intonation refers to the rise and fall of the pitch in our speech, and it plays a significant role in conveying meaning, emotions, and intentions. Whether you are a language learner or an educator in the field of language education, honing your intonation skills is essential to sound natural and effectively communicate your thoughts.

Intonation is like the melodic rhythm of language. It adds life, clarity, and expression to your words. By understanding and mastering intonation, you can enhance your overall spoken communication, make your sentences more engaging, and effectively convey your intended message.

To develop your intonation skills, it is crucial to listen attentively to native speakers and pay close attention to how they emphasize certain words or phrases. Observe the rise and fall in their pitch as they speak and try to replicate it in your own practice. Mimicking native speakers can help you internalize the natural rhythm and flow of the language.

Another effective way to improve your intonation is to engage in conversations with native speakers or language partners. By actively participating in real-life conversations, you can gain valuable exposure to different intonation patterns and learn to adapt your own speech accordingly. Practice asking questions, expressing emotions, and using intonation to create emphasis in your sentences.

Additionally, familiarize yourself with the concept of stress and its relation to intonation. Stress refers to the emphasis placed on certain syllables or words in a sentence. Understanding stress patterns is crucial for proper intonation, as it helps you convey the intended meaning and avoid miscommunication. Practice identifying and applying stress patterns in your speech to enhance your overall intonation skills.

Remember, developing intonation skills is a gradual process that requires patience and consistent practice. Regularly record your voice and listen back to identify areas for improvement. Utilize online resources, such as pronunciation exercises and intonation drills, to further enhance your skills.

By dedicating time and effort to developing your intonation skills, you will significantly enhance your spoken communication abilities. Whether you are a language learner seeking fluency or an educator aiming to enhance your teaching techniques, mastering intonation will enable you to communicate more effectively and confidently, ensuring that your message resonates with your audience.

Chapter 8: Common Pronunciation Mistakes

Mispronunciations of Vowel Sounds

In the vast world of language education, mastering pronunciation is often considered one of the most challenging tasks. Pronouncing words correctly requires understanding the intricacies of various vowel sounds, which can vary significantly across different languages. This subchapter, titled "Mispronunciations of Vowel Sounds," aims to address common errors made by learners of all backgrounds and provide valuable insights on perfecting vowel pronunciation.

Across languages, vowel sounds play a fundamental role in communication. However, mispronunciations of vowel sounds can lead to confusion and misunderstandings. To help you overcome these hurdles, this subchapter focuses on the most frequently mispronounced vowel sounds, shedding light on the reasons behind these errors and offering practical tips to rectify them.

One common mispronunciation is substituting one vowel sound for another due to the influence of one's native language. For instance, speakers of languages with a limited vowel inventory may struggle to differentiate between English vowel sounds such as /æ/ in "cat" and /ʌ/ in "cut." Understanding the unique characteristics of each vowel sound and practicing their correct pronunciation is essential in overcoming such challenges.

Another issue addressed in this subchapter is the misplacement of stress within words. Stress patterns can greatly impact vowel pronunciation. For instance, the word "export" has the primary stress on the second syllable, resulting in the vowel sound /ɔː/. Misplacing or neglecting stress can lead to mispronouncing the word as /ɛksˈpɔːrt/, altering the intended meaning.

Furthermore, certain vowel sounds are notoriously difficult for learners to produce accurately. The notorious schwa sound /ə/ often poses challenges as it appears in unstressed syllables and can easily be overlooked or replaced with a different vowel sound. Recognizing and practicing the schwa sound is crucial to achieving fluency and naturalness in pronunciation.

To assist you in perfecting your pronunciation, this subchapter provides a variety of exercises, including tongue twisters, minimal pairs, and listening activities. These exercises are designed to enhance your awareness of vowel sounds, improve your ability to differentiate between similar sounds, and ultimately strengthen your overall pronunciation skills.

Remember, mastering vowel sounds requires patience, practice, and a keen ear. By dedicating time and effort to this aspect of your language education, you will undoubtedly make significant strides towards achieving accurate and natural pronunciation. So, let's embark on this journey together and perfect our vowel sounds for effective communication!

In the realm of language education, mastering pronunciation is crucial for effective communication. Pronouncing vowel sounds accurately can be particularly challenging, as they vary across languages and dialects. Understanding and addressing common mispronunciations of vowel sounds can greatly enhance one's spoken language proficiency.

The English language, for instance, is notorious for its complex vowel system. Many learners struggle with distinguishing between similar vowel sounds, leading to misunderstandings and reduced clarity in speech. This subchapter aims to shed light on some of the most common mispronunciations of vowel sounds and provide practical strategies to perfect your pronunciation.

One frequently encountered issue is the mispronunciation of the short "i" sound (/ɪ/). This sound is often confused with the long "ee" sound (/iː/), resulting in miscommunications. By practicing minimal pairs exercises and paying close attention to mouth position and tongue placement, learners can develop the ability to differentiate between these two sounds.

Another challenge lies in pronouncing the schwa sound (/ə/), which frequently occurs in unstressed syllables. Due to its reduced prominence, learners often neglect or mispronounce it, leading to a lack of fluency and naturalness in speech. Raising awareness of the schwa sound and implementing drills to practice its correct production can significantly improve overall pronunciation skills.

The mispronunciation of diphthongs, such as the "ow" sound (/aʊ/) and the "oi" sound (/ɔɪ/), is also common among language learners. These diphthongs consist of a combination of two vowel sounds, and their accurate pronunciation requires attention to both the starting and ending points of the sound. Engaging in repetitive exercises and listening to native speakers can help learners internalize the correct production of these complex sounds.

Furthermore, regional accents and dialects can pose additional challenges in mastering vowel sounds. Different regions may have distinct vowel sounds that differ from the standard language. By immersing oneself in authentic materials, such as movies, songs, and podcasts, learners can expose themselves to various accents and train their ears to recognize and produce different vowel sounds accurately.

Perfecting your pronunciation of vowel sounds is a continuous process that requires patience and practice. By dedicating time to understanding and addressing common mispronunciations, learners can significantly enhance their language proficiency and become more confident and effective communicators.

In conclusion, this subchapter has explored some of the most common mispronunciations of vowel sounds and provided practical strategies for improvement. Remember, mastering pronunciation is a journey that requires dedication and perseverance. By continuously refining your vowel sounds, you will unlock the key to clearer and more accurate communication in any language.

Mispronunciations of Consonant Sounds

Consonant sounds play a crucial role in our everyday communication, and mastering their pronunciation is essential for effective language learning. However, mispronunciations of consonant sounds are a common challenge faced by learners of all ages and language backgrounds. In this subchapter, we will explore some of the most frequently mispronounced consonant sounds and provide you with practical tips on how to perfect your pronunciation.

One common mispronunciation is the distinction between the sounds of /th/ and /s/. Many non-native speakers struggle with differentiating these sounds, resulting in confusion and misunderstanding. The /th/ sound, like in "think" or "this," is produced by placing the tongue between the teeth and blowing air out gently. On the other hand, the /s/ sound, as in "seven" or "sun," is produced by pushing air through a narrow gap between the tongue and the roof of the mouth. Practice these sounds by repeating words that contain them and pay close attention to the position of your tongue and airflow.

Another mispronunciation involves the sounds /v/ and /w/. These sounds often get interchanged, leading to incorrect pronunciation. The /v/ sound, as in "victory" or "voice," is created by gently putting the bottom lip against the top teeth and releasing a continuous voiced sound. In contrast, the /w/ sound, like in "water" or "window," is produced by rounding the lips and creating a semi-vowel sound. Practice these sounds by pronouncing words that contain them, focusing on the lip position and voicing.

Additionally, the consonant sounds /r/ and /l/ pose a challenge for many learners. Non-native speakers tend to substitute one for the other, resulting in miscommunication. The /r/ sound, as in "rain" or "red," is produced by vibrating the tip of the tongue against the roof of the mouth. In contrast, the /l/ sound, like in "love" or "light," is produced by placing the tip of the tongue against the alveolar ridge. Practice these sounds by repeating words that contain them and pay attention to the tongue placement and vibration.

Mastering the correct pronunciation of consonant sounds is a vital step towards achieving clear and fluent communication in any language. By identifying and addressing common mispronunciations, you can significantly improve your language skills and enhance your overall language education experience.

Remember, practice makes perfect. Dedicate time each day to practice these consonant sounds, and listen to native speakers to refine your pronunciation further. By doing so, you will gain confidence, improve your communication skills, and truly perfect your pronunciation.

In the vast world of language education, one of the most common challenges learners face is mispronouncing certain consonant sounds. These mispronunciations often occur due to differences in native languages, resulting in difficulties in achieving perfect pronunciation. However, fear not, as this subchapter aims to provide a comprehensive guide to help everyone perfect their pronunciation skills.

The English language is known for its complex consonant sounds, and mastering them can significantly enhance your fluency and clarity.

Let's explore some of the most frequently mispronounced consonant sounds and learn how to overcome these challenges.

Firstly, the "th" sound, as in "think" and "this," can be particularly troublesome for non-native speakers. Many mistakenly substitute it with a "d" or "s" sound. To improve your pronunciation, practice placing your tongue between your teeth, lightly blowing air, and producing a soft "th" sound.

Another common error is mispronouncing the "r" sound. Many learners tend to roll or trill their tongues, resulting in a distorted sound. To overcome this, practice placing the tip of your tongue near your upper teeth and lightly tap it to create a soft, unrolled "r" sound.

Additionally, the "v" and "w" sounds often cause confusion. Non-native speakers may substitute one for the other, leading to misunderstandings. To differentiate between the two, practice pronouncing the "v" sound by gently biting your lower lip with your upper teeth while simultaneously vibrating your vocal cords. For the "w" sound, round your lips and produce a sound similar to blowing out a candle.

Lastly, the "p" and "b" sounds can be challenging due to the subtle differences in voicing. Many learners struggle with distinguishing between the two, resulting in words being misunderstood. To improve this, practice producing the "p" sound by closing your lips firmly and releasing a small burst of air. For the "b" sound, create the same lip closure but engage your vocal cords to produce a voiced sound.

Remember, perfecting your pronunciation takes time and practice. By focusing on these commonly mispronounced consonant sounds, you can significantly enhance your language skills and communicate more effectively. Embrace the challenge, dedicate yourself to practice, and soon, you will master these sounds with confidence.

In conclusion, this subchapter has addressed some of the most frequently mispronounced consonant sounds encountered in language education. By understanding the correct techniques and practicing these sounds, everyone can perfect their pronunciation skills and improve their fluency. So, don't be discouraged by mispronunciations; instead, embrace the opportunity to learn and grow. Happy practicing!

Common Stress and Rhythm Errors

Proper pronunciation is essential when it comes to effective communication. However, many language learners struggle with stress and rhythm, leading to misunderstandings and difficulty in conveying their intended message. In this subchapter, we will explore some of the most common stress and rhythm errors made by language learners and provide strategies to help you perfect your pronunciation.

Stress refers to the emphasis placed on certain syllables within a word or sentence. In many languages, including English, stress patterns play a crucial role in conveying meaning. Incorrectly placing stress on syllables can result in words being misunderstood or sounding unnatural. One common error is placing stress on the wrong syllable in multi-syllabic words. For example, pronouncing "photograph" as "PHO-to-graph" instead of "pho-TO-graph." To overcome this error, it is essential to understand the stress patterns of the language you are learning and practice with native speakers or pronunciation guides.

Rhythm, on the other hand, refers to the timing and flow of speech. Many learners struggle with maintaining the appropriate rhythm, leading to speech that sounds robotic or disjointed. One common error is speaking too slowly or too quickly, disrupting the natural rhythm of the language. To improve your rhythm, try listening to native speakers and imitating their pace and intonation. Record yourself speaking and compare it to a native speaker to identify any discrepancies. Practicing rhythmic exercises, such as reading poetry or singing along with songs, can also help you develop a more natural flow in your speech.

Another common error is failing to recognize and use the correct stress and rhythm patterns in phrases and sentences. Stress patterns can change depending on the part of speech or the function of a word in a sentence. For instance, the stress in the noun form of "record" is on the first syllable ("RE-cord"), while the verb form emphasizes the second syllable ("re-CORD"). By understanding these patterns and practicing sentence-level stress and rhythm exercises, you can enhance your overall pronunciation and make your speech more fluent and natural.

In conclusion, proper stress and rhythm are crucial components of pronunciation that can greatly impact your ability to communicate effectively. By understanding the common errors associated with stress and rhythm and implementing the strategies provided, you can perfect your pronunciation and improve your overall language proficiency. Remember, practice is key, so make a conscious effort to incorporate stress and rhythm exercises into your language learning routine.

Title: Common Stress and Rhythm Errors

Introduction:
In the realm of language education, mastering pronunciation is a crucial aspect of effective communication. However, many individuals struggle with common stress and rhythm errors, hindering their ability to convey their message clearly. In this subchapter of "Perfecting Your Pronunciation: A Comprehensive Guide for Everyone," we will delve into these common errors and provide you with practical strategies to overcome them.

Understanding   Stress   Errors:
One of the most common stress errors occurs when we place emphasis on the wrong syllable of a word. This misplacement can lead to misunderstanding and confusion. To address this issue, we will explore stress patterns within different languages and provide exercises to help you internalize correct stress placement.

Mastering   Rhythm:
Rhythm is another critical aspect of pronunciation that can greatly impact how well you are understood. The rhythm of a language refers to the pattern of stressed and unstressed syllables within words and sentences. Many individuals struggle with maintaining the appropriate rhythm, leading to a stilted or unnatural speech pattern. In this subchapter, we will break down rhythm errors and offer techniques to improve your rhythmical fluency.

Techniques   to   Improve   Stress   and   Rhythm:
Perfecting stress and rhythm requires practice and dedication. We will outline various techniques that can significantly enhance your pronunciation skills. These techniques include:

1. Listening to native speakers: Immersing yourself in authentic language samples allows you to develop an innate sense of stress and rhythm patterns.

2. Shadowing exercises: By imitating native speakers, you can train your ear and mouth to replicate natural stress and rhythm.

3. Clapping or tapping exercises: These physical activities help develop a kinesthetic awareness of stress and rhythm patterns.

4. Reading aloud: Practicing stress and rhythm through reading exercises allows you to identify and correct errors in real-time.

Conclusion:

Common stress and rhythm errors can hinder effective communication and understanding. However, with the right techniques and practice, you can overcome these obstacles and perfect your pronunciation skills. By focusing on stress patterns, mastering rhythm, and employing various techniques outlined in this subchapter, you will be well on your way to attaining clear and confident pronunciation. Remember, consistent effort and dedication are key to achieving success in language education.

Overcoming Pronunciation Challenges

Pronunciation plays a vital role in effective communication, regardless of the language we speak. However, mastering the correct pronunciation can be a challenging endeavor. Whether you are a native speaker or a language learner, Perfecting Your Pronunciation: A Comprehensive Guide for Everyone aims to provide you with valuable insights and strategies to overcome pronunciation challenges.

One common obstacle many individuals face is the difficulty in pronouncing sounds that are not present in their native language. It can be frustrating when you are unable to articulate certain sounds correctly, leading to misunderstandings and miscommunications. This subchapter will equip you with techniques and exercises to tackle these pronunciation hurdles head-on.

To begin, it is crucial to understand the phonetic structure of the language you are learning. Familiarize yourself with its unique sounds and phonemes, as well as their corresponding symbols. By developing a solid foundation in phonetics, you will be better equipped to identify and pronounce unfamiliar sounds accurately.

Another effective strategy is to immerse yourself in the language. Listen to native speakers, whether through audio recordings, podcasts, or even by watching movies or TV shows. Pay close attention to their pronunciation, intonation, and stress patterns. Mimicking their speech will help you internalize the correct pronunciation and natural rhythm of the language.

Furthermore, practicing pronunciation exercises regularly is essential for improvement. Perfecting Your Pronunciation offers a wide range of exercises tailored to specific sounds and pronunciation challenges. From tongue twisters to minimal pairs, these exercises will help you train your vocal apparatus and refine your pronunciation skills.

Additionally, seeking feedback from a language tutor or participating in language exchange programs can greatly enhance your progress. A qualified tutor can provide personalized guidance and correct any pronunciation errors you may be making. Meanwhile, engaging in conversations with native speakers will expose you to real-life situations and help you adapt your pronunciation in different contexts.

Remember, overcoming pronunciation challenges requires patience and perseverance. It is a gradual process that requires consistent practice and dedication. However, with the right tools and strategies outlined in Perfecting Your Pronunciation: A Comprehensive Guide for Everyone, you can conquer these obstacles and achieve clear and confident communication in any language.

So, whether you are a language learner or simply interested in improving your pronunciation, this subchapter will equip you with the necessary tools to overcome pronunciation challenges and enhance your language skills. Embrace the journey towards perfecting your pronunciation, and unlock the doors to effective communication in the realm of language education.

In the vast world of language education, one of the most common hurdles that learners face is mastering pronunciation. Whether you are learning a new language or striving to polish your skills in a familiar one, Perfecting Your Pronunciation: A Comprehensive Guide for Everyone is here to help you overcome these challenges.

Pronunciation plays a vital role in effective communication. It enables you to express your thoughts clearly, be understood by native speakers, and build confidence in your language abilities. However, pronouncing words accurately can be a daunting task due to various factors such as unfamiliar sounds, different phonetic rules, and regional accents. This subchapter aims to equip you with valuable techniques and strategies to overcome these hurdles and improve your pronunciation skills.

Firstly, it is essential to understand the specific challenges you may encounter. Different languages have distinct phonetic systems, which means that certain sounds may not exist in your native language. Identifying these sounds and practicing them through phonetic exercises will help you acquire the necessary muscle memory to reproduce them accurately. By focusing on individual sounds, you can gradually overcome pronunciation difficulties.

Another hurdle to overcome is the influence of regional accents. Native speakers often have distinct accents, which may make it challenging for non-native speakers to understand and imitate. Exposure to a variety of accents and dialects through authentic audio and video resources can help familiarize yourself with these variations. Additionally, mimicking native speakers' intonation, stress patterns, and rhythm can significantly enhance your pronunciation skills.

Moreover, integrating technology into your language learning journey can be immensely beneficial. Utilizing pronunciation apps, speech recognition software, and online resources allows you to receive instant feedback on your pronunciation. These tools can provide valuable insights into areas that need improvement, making your practice sessions more efficient and targeted.

Furthermore, actively engaging in conversation with native speakers or language exchange partners can immensely improve your pronunciation skills. Regular interaction with individuals who can provide constructive feedback and correct your mistakes will help you refine your pronunciation and gain fluency. Additionally, joining language communities or attending language workshops can provide a supportive environment for practicing and receiving guidance.

In conclusion, overcoming pronunciation challenges is an integral part of language education. Perfecting Your Pronunciation: A Comprehensive Guide for Everyone aims to equip learners with effective techniques to tackle these hurdles. By understanding the specific challenges you may face, exposing yourself to a variety of accents, utilizing technology, and actively engaging with native speakers, you can enhance your pronunciation skills and become a confident and proficient communicator. So, let's embark on this pronunciation journey together and pave the way for successful language learning!

Chapter 9: Strategies for Improvement

Listening to Native Speakers

Subchapter: Listening to Native Speakers

Introduction:
Listening to native speakers is an essential component of perfecting your pronunciation and becoming fluent in any language. By immersing yourself in the sounds, rhythms, and intonations of native speakers, you will develop a better understanding of the language and refine your own pronunciation skills. In this subchapter, we will explore various strategies and techniques to help you effectively listen to native speakers and improve your overall language proficiency.

1.   Active   Listening:
Listening actively involves being fully engaged and focused on the speaker's words, tone, and pronunciation. Avoid passive listening, where you simply let the sounds wash over you without actively processing them. Actively listen by paying attention to the speaker's articulation, stress patterns, and subtle nuances in pronunciation. Take note of any unfamiliar words or phrases and try to understand their usage in context.

2.   Mimicking   Native   Speakers:
One of the most effective ways to improve your pronunciation is by mimicking native speakers. Listen to recordings of native speakers and repeat what they say, trying to match their intonation, rhythm, and cadence. Pay attention to how they form sounds and syllables, and

practice imitating them. This technique helps develop muscle memory and trains your mouth to produce authentic sounds.

3.   Shadowing   Technique:
The shadowing technique involves listening to native speakers while simultaneously speaking along with them. This method helps synchronize your speech with the natural flow and rhythm of the language. Start with short phrases or sentences and gradually increase the complexity as you become more comfortable. By shadowing native speakers, you will enhance your pronunciation and fluency.

4.   Immersion   and   Authentic   Materials:
Immerse yourself in the language by surrounding yourself with authentic materials such as movies, TV shows, podcasts, and music in the target language. Exposure to native speakers in real-life contexts will help you understand the natural flow of the language and expose you to various accents and dialects. Regularly listening to authentic materials will train your ear to recognize and reproduce the sounds accurately.

5.   Utilize   Technology:
Take advantage of technology to enhance your listening skills. Use language learning apps, online platforms, and podcasts specifically designed to improve your listening comprehension. These resources often provide exercises and activities to help you practice understanding native speakers.

Conclusion:
Listening to native speakers is a vital aspect of language education. By actively engaging with authentic materials, mimicking native speakers,

and utilizing technology, you can perfect your pronunciation and achieve fluency in the language. Embrace the opportunity to listen to native speakers as it will greatly enhance your overall language proficiency and communication skills.

In the journey of perfecting your pronunciation, one crucial aspect that cannot be overlooked is listening to native speakers. Immersing yourself in the natural rhythms, intonations, and accents of a language is invaluable for developing an authentic and accurate pronunciation. This subchapter will explore the importance of listening to native speakers and provide practical tips to help you make the most of this essential language education tool.

Listening to native speakers not only exposes you to the correct pronunciation of words, but it also familiarizes you with the nuances, phrasing, and cultural context of the language. By listening to authentic conversations, interviews, and speeches, you gain a deeper understanding of how words are used in real-life situations.

To make the most of your listening practice, it is advisable to expose yourself to a variety of native speakers. Different regions and dialects within a language can have distinct pronunciations and accents. By listening to a diverse range of native speakers, you can broaden your understanding and adaptability to different speech patterns.

Additionally, technology has made it easier than ever to access native audio content. Utilize language learning apps, podcasts, online videos, and audiobooks to immerse yourself in the language. These resources often provide transcripts or subtitles to help you follow along and understand unfamiliar words or phrases.

While listening to native speakers, it is essential to actively engage with the content. Pay attention to the speaker's intonation, stress, and rhythm. Notice how certain sounds are produced and practice mimicking them. Regularly listen to the same audio material multiple times to reinforce your understanding and improve your pronunciation.

To further enhance your listening skills, consider participating in language exchange programs or finding conversation partners who are native speakers. Engaging in conversations with native speakers allows you to practice pronunciation in a natural, interactive setting. It also provides an opportunity to receive feedback and guidance from someone who possesses a deep understanding of the language.

Listening to native speakers is a powerful tool for language education. It helps you internalize the correct pronunciation, familiarize yourself with various accents, and develop an authentic speaking style. Embrace the opportunity to immerse yourself in the language through audio materials, conversations, and interactions with native speakers. By actively listening and practicing, you will steadily perfect your pronunciation and become a more fluent and confident speaker.

Mimicking Native Pronunciation

In the realm of language education, one crucial aspect that often gets overlooked is achieving native-like pronunciation. Perfecting Your Pronunciation: A Comprehensive Guide for Everyone recognizes the significance of this skill and aims to equip language learners with the tools and strategies needed to mimic native pronunciation.

Whether you are a beginner or an advanced learner, acquiring native-like pronunciation is essential for effective communication. Native speakers are often more receptive and understanding when they encounter learners who can pronounce words and phrases accurately. It creates a sense of connection and builds confidence in your language abilities.

This subchapter delves into the techniques and methods that can help you mimic native pronunciation. It emphasizes the importance of listening and observing native speakers in order to grasp the subtle nuances of their speech patterns. By immersing yourself in the language and culture, you can develop a better understanding of how to pronounce words authentically.

One effective technique discussed in this subchapter is shadowing. This method involves listening to native speakers and repeating their words and phrases simultaneously. By doing so, you can practice mimicking their intonation, stress, rhythm, and overall pronunciation. Regular shadowing exercises can significantly enhance your ability to imitate native speakers.

The subchapter also explores the significance of phonetics and phonology. Understanding the phonetic symbols and sounds of a language is crucial for accurate pronunciation. By familiarizing yourself with the phonetic inventory of your target language, you can identify the sounds that are different from your native language and work on mastering them. Additionally, studying the phonological rules and patterns of a language can help you understand why certain sounds are pronounced in specific ways.

Perfecting Your Pronunciation: A Comprehensive Guide for Everyone provides practical exercises and activities to assist you in improving your pronunciation skills. It emphasizes the importance of consistent practice and offers tips to overcome common pronunciation challenges. By dedicating time and effort to mimic native pronunciation, you can enhance your language abilities and communicate more effectively with native speakers.

Regardless of your language proficiency level, Perfecting Your Pronunciation: A Comprehensive Guide for Everyone is an invaluable resource for anyone seeking to achieve native-like pronunciation. With its comprehensive approach and practical strategies, this book is a must-have for language learners who aspire to communicate with confidence and authenticity.

Subchapter: Mimicking Native Pronunciation

Perfecting Your Pronunciation: A Comprehensive Guide for Everyone

Language Education

In the pursuit of language mastery, pronunciation plays a vital role in effectively conveying meaning and connecting with native speakers. Achieving native-like pronunciation may seem daunting, but with dedication and the right techniques, anyone can improve their pronunciation skills. This subchapter aims to guide you through the process of mimicking native pronunciation, helping you sound more natural and confident in your target language.

1. Understanding the Importance of Native Pronunciation: Native speakers often have an intuitive understanding of the rhythm, stress, and intonation patterns of their language. By mimicking their pronunciation, you can communicate more effectively and be better understood. Additionally, native-like pronunciation can boost your confidence and help you integrate into new linguistic and cultural environments seamlessly.

2. Listening and Repetition: Immersing yourself in the language is crucial. Listen attentively to native speakers, whether through audio recordings, podcasts, or conversations. Pay close attention to the sounds, stress patterns, and intonation they use. Then, practice repeating what you hear, aiming to match their tone and rhythm. Regular practice will help train your ears and vocal muscles to produce more accurate sounds.

3.   Phonetics   and   Pronunciation   Guides: Understanding the phonetic system of your target language can greatly assist in mimicking native pronunciation. Learn about the specific sounds, phonemes, and phonetic rules of the language. Utilize pronunciation guides, dictionaries, and online resources that provide audio samples and detailed explanations. Practice pronouncing words using the correct phonetic representations.

4.   Mouth   and   Tongue   Placement: Each language has its unique set of sounds, and mimicking native pronunciation involves mastering these sounds. Pay attention to where your mouth, tongue, and lips are positioned while producing different sounds. Practice exercises that target specific sounds, such as tongue twisters or minimal pairs, to improve your articulation.

5.   Record   and   Evaluate: Recording yourself speaking in the target language is an excellent way to assess your progress. Compare your pronunciation with that of native speakers, noting areas where you need improvement. Listen for specific sounds, stress patterns, or intonation variations that may be different from your own pronunciation. Continually refine your skills by re-recording and analyzing your speech.

Remember, achieving native-like pronunciation takes time and effort. Embrace the journey, be patient with yourself, and celebrate small victories along the way. By mimicking native pronunciation, you will enhance your language proficiency, connect with native speakers, and confidently express yourself in your chosen language.

Recording and Analyzing Your Speech

In the quest to perfect your pronunciation, recording and analyzing your speech is an invaluable technique that can greatly enhance your language learning journey. By capturing your own voice and critically examining it, you can identify areas of improvement, work on specific sounds, and ultimately achieve clearer and more accurate speech.

Recording your voice is a simple process that can be done with readily available tools such as smartphones or digital recorders. Find a quiet space where you feel comfortable speaking, and start by reading aloud a passage or practicing certain sounds or words. It is essential to relax and speak naturally to get an accurate representation of your speech patterns.

Once you have recorded your speech, it's time to analyze it. This can be done by listening to the recording or using software applications specifically designed for language education purposes. When listening to your recording, pay close attention to the clarity, pronunciation, and intonation of your speech. Take note of any areas where you stumble or struggle with certain sounds. Are there any words or phrases that are consistently pronounced incorrectly? Are you speaking too fast or too slow? Analyzing these aspects will help you identify your strengths and weaknesses, allowing you to focus on areas that need improvement.

To further enhance your analysis, consider seeking feedback from native speakers or language instructors. They can provide valuable insights and point out specific areas that require attention. Additionally, there are online communities and language exchange platforms where you can share your recordings and receive constructive feedback from fellow language learners.

Once you have identified the areas that need improvement, it's time to practice. Repeat the words or sounds that you struggle with, focusing on proper pronunciation and intonation. Practice them in isolation and then incorporate them into sentences and conversations. It's important to practice consistently and be patient with yourself as progress takes time.

Recording and analyzing your speech is not only a useful technique for identifying areas of improvement but also a motivating tool to track your progress. By comparing your recordings from different points in your language learning journey, you will be able to observe the advancements you have made. This sense of progress will boost your confidence and keep you motivated to continue perfecting your pronunciation.

In conclusion, recording and analyzing your speech is a powerful tool in perfecting your pronunciation. It allows you to identify areas of improvement, practice specific sounds, and track your progress. By incorporating this technique into your language learning routine, you will be well on your way to achieving clearer and more accurate speech. So grab a recording device, start analyzing, and embark on your journey to perfect pronunciation !

In the journey of perfecting your pronunciation, recording and analyzing your speech is an essential step towards achieving your goals. By utilizing modern technology and adopting effective techniques, you can gain a deeper understanding of your strengths and weaknesses when it comes to pronouncing different sounds and words. This subchapter will guide you through the process of recording and analyzing your speech, providing you with valuable insights to improve your pronunciation.

Recording your speech allows you to listen to your own voice objectively, enabling you to identify areas that need improvement. With the advancement of smartphones and other recording devices, it has become incredibly easy to record yourself speaking in various situations. Whether you are practicing alone or engaging in a conversation with a native speaker, make it a habit to record yourself regularly. This will provide you with an ample amount of material to analyze and work on.

Once you have recorded your speech, it is time to analyze it. Start by listening to the recording attentively, focusing on specific sounds, words, or phrases that you find challenging. Pay close attention to your intonation, stress patterns, and any other aspects of pronunciation that you aim to improve. Take notes on the areas that need attention and make a list of words or sounds that you want to practice further.

To enhance your analysis, consider using specialized software or mobile applications designed for language education. These tools can provide visual representations of your speech patterns, highlighting areas where you may be struggling. Some applications even offer interactive exercises and tutorials to help you target specific pronunciation difficulties. Utilize these resources to gain a comprehensive understanding of your pronunciation strengths and weaknesses.

Additionally, seek feedback from others who are proficient in the language you are learning. Share your recordings with native speakers or language teachers who can provide valuable insights and suggestions for improvement. Engage in conversations with them, focusing on the specific areas you want to work on. This will allow you to receive real-time feedback and make necessary adjustments.

Recording and analyzing your speech is a powerful tool in perfecting your pronunciation. By incorporating this practice into your language learning routine, you will develop a heightened awareness of your speech patterns and make significant strides towards achieving clearer and more accurate pronunciation. Embrace this process, and you will see remarkable progress in your language skills.

Seeking Feedback and Guidance

In the journey towards perfecting your pronunciation, seeking feedback and guidance plays a crucial role. It is an essential step that allows you to identify areas for improvement and refine your pronunciation skills. This subchapter will delve into the importance of seeking feedback and guidance, and provide you with valuable tips on how to do so effectively.

Feedback is the key to progress. Without it, you may remain unaware of the errors and nuances that hinder your pronunciation. Seeking feedback helps you gain insights into your strengths and weaknesses, enabling you to focus on specific areas that require attention. Whether you are a language learner, teacher, or someone looking to enhance their communication skills, feedback is invaluable.

To seek feedback effectively, it is essential to create a supportive and constructive environment. Encourage friends, family, or colleagues to provide honest feedback without fear of judgment. You can also join language exchange programs or conversation groups where you can practice your pronunciation and receive guidance from native speakers or experienced language learners.

Another valuable resource for seeking feedback is online platforms and forums dedicated to language education. These platforms provide opportunities to connect with language enthusiasts and professionals from all around the world. You can share recordings of your pronunciation and receive feedback from a diverse range of individuals with different linguistic backgrounds.

When seeking feedback, it is crucial to be open-minded and receptive to suggestions. Embrace feedback as a tool for growth rather than taking it personally. Remember, the goal is to improve your pronunciation, and constructive criticism is an integral part of the learning process.

In addition to seeking feedback, guidance is equally important in perfecting your pronunciation. Guidance can come from various sources, including language teachers, pronunciation experts, or even self-help resources. Seek out materials such as pronunciation guides, audio resources, and online tutorials that offer step-by-step instructions and exercises to help you refine your pronunciation.

Language education programs or courses specifically designed to address pronunciation can also be immensely beneficial. These programs provide structured guidance, focusing on the different aspects of pronunciation, such as intonation, stress, and vowel sounds. They often incorporate interactive exercises and provide personalized feedback to facilitate your pronunciation improvement.

In conclusion, seeking feedback and guidance is paramount when perfecting your pronunciation. Embrace feedback as an opportunity for growth and improvement, and actively seek guidance from various sources. By doing so, you will enhance your pronunciation skills, communicate more effectively, and gain confidence in your language abilities. Remember, perfecting pronunciation is a lifelong journey, and feedback and guidance are your trusted companions along the way.

In the journey of perfecting your pronunciation, seeking feedback and guidance from others plays a crucial role. Whether you are a language learner, an educator, or simply someone interested in improving your pronunciation skills, receiving constructive feedback and guidance can significantly enhance your progress and help you achieve your goals.

Feedback from others provides an external perspective on your pronunciation, offering valuable insights into areas that need improvement. It allows you to identify and rectify any pronunciation errors or habits that may hinder effective communication. Seeking feedback from native speakers or qualified language instructors can offer you a more accurate assessment of your pronunciation, helping you fine-tune your skills and sound more natural in your target language.

One of the most effective ways to seek feedback is through conversation partners or language exchange programs. Engaging in conversations with native speakers or fellow language learners not only provides an opportunity to practice your pronunciation but also allows you to receive real-time feedback and guidance. They can help you identify specific sounds or intonation patterns that require attention, as well as offer suggestions on how to improve them.

Another valuable source of feedback and guidance is through technology. Nowadays, numerous pronunciation apps and software programs are available that can analyze your pronunciation and provide instant feedback. These tools use advanced algorithms to detect specific pronunciation errors and offer detailed insights on how to correct them. Incorporating these technological resources into your language learning routine can help you monitor your progress, identify areas for improvement, and practice pronunciation exercises tailored to your needs.

However, seeking feedback and guidance should not be limited to external sources alone. Self-evaluation is equally important. Recording yourself while speaking or reading aloud allows you to listen back and objectively assess your own pronunciation. By comparing your recordings to native speakers or audio samples, you can identify any discrepancies and make the necessary adjustments. Keeping a journal to track your progress and noting areas where you need further practice can also be beneficial.

In conclusion, seeking feedback and guidance is essential for perfecting your pronunciation skills. Whether you rely on conversations with native speakers, language exchange programs, technology, or self-evaluation, incorporating feedback into your language learning routine will accelerate your progress and help you achieve fluency. So, embrace the opportunity to receive constructive feedback and guidance, and watch your pronunciation skills soar.

Incorporating Pronunciation in Daily Life

Pronunciation is a crucial aspect of language learning, yet it often gets overlooked or neglected. Many language learners focus solely on vocabulary and grammar, forgetting that clear and accurate pronunciation is essential for effective communication. In this subchapter, we will explore various ways to incorporate pronunciation practice into your daily life, helping you perfect your pronunciation skills and become a confident communicator.

One effective way to improve your pronunciation is through listening to native speakers. Make it a habit to listen to podcasts, watch movies or TV shows, and listen to music in the target language. Pay attention to the sounds, intonation, and rhythm of the language. Mimic the pronunciation and try to imitate the native speakers as closely as possible. By constantly exposing yourself to authentic language, you will gradually internalize the correct pronunciation patterns.

Another useful technique is to practice pronunciation exercises regularly. Set aside a few minutes each day to work on specific sounds, words, or phrases that you find challenging. You can find pronunciation exercises and resources online or use language learning apps that offer pronunciation practice features. Remember to focus on individual sounds, stress patterns, and word linking to improve your overall pronunciation.

Incorporating pronunciation into your daily routine is also crucial. Whenever you speak in the target language, be mindful of your pronunciation. Pay attention to how you articulate each sound and try to correct any mistakes you notice. Practice speaking with native speakers or language exchange partners who can provide feedback and help you improve. Additionally, record yourself speaking and listen to the recordings to identify areas that need improvement.

Using pronunciation guides and dictionaries can also be beneficial. When learning new words, refer to pronunciation guides or listen to audio recordings to ensure you are pronouncing them correctly. Make a habit of looking up unfamiliar words in a dictionary that provides phonetic transcriptions. This will help you avoid developing incorrect pronunciation habits.

Lastly, don't be afraid to make mistakes. Pronunciation is a skill that requires practice and patience. Embrace the learning process and be open to feedback. Remember that it's better to make mistakes and learn from them than to stay silent out of fear of mispronunciation.

Incorporating pronunciation practice into your daily life is essential for improving your language skills. By listening to native speakers, regularly practicing pronunciation exercises, being mindful of your pronunciation in daily conversations, using pronunciation guides, and embracing mistakes, you will make significant progress in perfecting your pronunciation and becoming a confident communicator in your target language.

Pronunciation plays a crucial role in effective communication. It helps convey our thoughts clearly, leaving no room for misinterpretation. By incorporating pronunciation practice into your daily life, you can improve your language skills and enhance your overall communication abilities. This subchapter explores various techniques and strategies to help you perfect your pronunciation effortlessly.

One effective way to incorporate pronunciation in your daily routine is by listening to native speakers. Expose yourself to authentic audio materials such as podcasts, audiobooks, or even conversations with native speakers. Pay attention to their intonation, stress patterns, and rhythm. By imitating their speech patterns, you can internalize the correct pronunciation and gradually integrate it into your own speech.

Another useful technique is shadowing. This involves listening to a native speaker and simultaneously repeating what they say. By actively mimicking their pronunciation, you can train your mouth muscles to produce the correct sounds. This technique not only improves your pronunciation but also enhances your listening skills and overall fluency.

Practicing pronunciation through tongue twisters is another fun and effective way to incorporate it into your daily life. Tongue twisters are challenging phrases that contain a series of similar sounds or difficult combinations. By regularly practicing these tongue twisters, you can train your tongue and mouth muscles to enunciate words clearly and accurately.

Additionally, self-recording is an invaluable tool for improving your pronunciation. Use your smartphone or any recording device to capture your speech. Listen to your recordings and compare them with native speakers. Take note of any differences and make necessary adjustments. This self-awareness will help you identify and correct any pronunciation errors.

Lastly, join language exchange groups or conversation clubs in your community. Engaging in conversations with other language learners or native speakers provides you with a supportive environment to practice your pronunciation. Encourage constructive feedback from others, as it will further refine your pronunciation skills.

Incorporating pronunciation practice into your daily life is essential for achieving fluency and effective communication. By listening to native speakers, shadowing, practicing tongue twisters, self-recording, and engaging in conversation clubs, you can gradually perfect your pronunciation skills. Remember, consistent practice and patience are key to mastering pronunciation and enhancing your overall language abilities.

Chapter 10: Accent Reduction Techniques

Understanding Accents and Dialects

In our increasingly interconnected world, the ability to communicate effectively with people from different cultures and backgrounds is becoming more important than ever. Language education plays a crucial role in facilitating this communication, and one aspect that often poses a challenge is understanding accents and dialects. This subchapter aims to provide a comprehensive guide for individuals seeking to perfect their pronunciation and enhance their ability to comprehend diverse accents and dialects.

Accents and dialects are natural variations in pronunciation and vocabulary that arise within a language due to geographical, cultural, and social factors. They add richness and diversity to our linguistic landscape, reflecting the unique histories and identities of different communities. However, they can also pose difficulties for learners, as they require adjusting to unfamiliar speech patterns and vocabulary.

The first step in understanding accents and dialects is to develop active listening skills. By actively listening to native speakers and exposing oneself to a variety of accents, learners can familiarize themselves with the sounds, rhythms, and intonations specific to different dialects. This exposure can be achieved through engaging with authentic audio materials, such as podcasts, music, movies, and news broadcasts.

Next, learners should focus on recognizing and understanding common phonetic features of different accents. This includes identifying vowel and consonant sounds that may differ from the learner's native language or standard dialect. By practicing these sounds and paying attention to their specific articulation, learners can improve their ability to perceive and reproduce them accurately.

Moreover, understanding the cultural context and linguistic history of a particular accent or dialect can also enhance comprehension. By delving into the socio-cultural aspects of a language, learners can gain insights into the unique vocabulary, idiomatic expressions, and grammatical structures used by speakers of different dialects.

Lastly, it is important to approach accents and dialects with an open mind and without judgment. Being respectful and appreciative of the diversity of languages and cultures will foster positive communication experiences. By embracing accents and dialects as valuable elements of language, learners can forge meaningful connections and overcome barriers in their language education journey.

In conclusion, understanding accents and dialects is a vital aspect of language education. By actively listening, familiarizing oneself with phonetic features, exploring cultural context, and maintaining an open mindset, learners can develop a comprehensive understanding of diverse accents and dialects. This subchapter aims to equip individuals with the necessary tools to navigate the intricacies of accent and dialect comprehension, ultimately enhancing their overall communication skills.

Accents and dialects play a significant role in communication, shaping the way we express ourselves and understand others. In this subchapter, we will delve into the fascinating world of accents and dialects, exploring their importance in language education.

Accents and dialects are variations in pronunciation, vocabulary, and grammar that occur in different regions or social groups. They reflect the unique cultural and historical backgrounds of speakers and contribute to the diversity of languages worldwide. While accents refer to the way words are pronounced, dialects encompass broader linguistic features, including vocabulary and grammar.

One key aspect of understanding accents and dialects is recognizing that they are neither right nor wrong. They are simply different ways of speaking within a language. Unfortunately, accents and dialects often carry certain stigmas, leading to misconceptions or prejudices. By learning about and appreciating different accents and dialects, we can improve our communication skills and foster inclusivity.

Language education plays a vital role in understanding and appreciating accents and dialects. When learning a new language, it is important to expose oneself to various accents and dialects to develop a well-rounded understanding. This exposure helps learners become more adaptable in different linguistic contexts and enhances their ability to communicate effectively with native speakers from diverse backgrounds.

Furthermore, understanding accents and dialects can help individuals become better listeners. By recognizing and interpreting different pronunciations and speech patterns, we can comprehend spoken language more accurately and improve our overall language skills. This skill is particularly important in today's globalized world, where international communication is increasingly common.

In this subchapter, we will explore different accents and dialects within various languages, providing examples and exercises to help readers tune their ears to different sounds and speech patterns. We will discuss the impact of accents on pronunciation and provide strategies to improve comprehension and pronunciation in different accents.

By the end of this subchapter, readers will gain a deeper understanding of the significance of accents and dialects in language education. They will be equipped with tools and techniques to navigate the rich tapestry of linguistic diversity, enhancing their communication skills and fostering a greater appreciation for the global community they are a part of.

Remember, accents and dialects are not barriers but gateways to broader cultural understanding and connection. Embrace the richness they offer, and let us embark on this exciting journey together in perfecting our pronunciation and expanding our linguistic horizons.

Techniques for Accent Reduction

Having a strong command over pronunciation is crucial for effective communication, especially in today's globalized world. Accents can often hinder one's ability to be understood clearly, leading to misunderstandings and misinterpretations. However, with the right techniques and consistent practice, anyone can work towards reducing their accent and perfecting their pronunciation.

1. Phonetics and Phonology: Understanding the basic principles of phonetics and phonology is the first step towards accent reduction. Familiarize yourself with the sounds of the target language and learn to differentiate between similar sounds. This knowledge will enable you to identify and correct specific pronunciation errors.

2. Mimic Native Speakers: Listen to native speakers of the language you want to improve your pronunciation in. Pay attention to their intonation, stress patterns, and rhythm. Practice imitating their speech patterns to internalize correct pronunciation.

3. Record and Analyze: Use a recording device to record yourself speaking in the target language. Listen to the recordings and compare them to native speakers. Identify areas where your pronunciation deviates from the native speakers and work on improving those specific sounds or patterns.

4. Tongue Twisters and Minimal Pairs: Engage in tongue twisters and minimal pair exercises to improve your pronunciation. These exercises focus on similar sounds that are often mispronounced. By repeatedly practicing these exercises, you can train your tongue and mouth muscles to produce accurate sounds.

5. Speech Therapy Apps: Utilize technology to your advantage. Several speech therapy apps offer exercises and interactive activities to help improve pronunciation. These apps provide instant feedback, allowing you to track your progress and focus on specific problem areas.

6. Enroll in Pronunciation Classes: Consider enrolling in a pronunciation class or seeking guidance from a language tutor. A professional instructor can identify your specific accent-related challenges and guide you through personalized exercises and techniques for improvement.

7. Practice Regularly: Consistency is key when it comes to accent reduction. Set aside dedicated practice time every day, even if it's only for a few minutes. Regular practice will help you build muscle memory and reinforce correct pronunciation habits.

Remember, accent reduction is a gradual process, and it requires patience, dedication, and perseverance. Embrace your journey and celebrate small victories along the way. By employing these techniques and committing to regular practice, you can perfect your pronunciation and enhance your overall language skills.

In today's globalized world, effective communication is crucial, particularly in the realm of language education. Whether you're a non-native English speaker striving to improve your pronunciation or a language teacher helping students refine their speech, accent reduction is a valuable skill. This subchapter aims to equip readers with a range of techniques to perfect their pronunciation and reduce accent-related barriers in communication.

1. Phonetics and Phonology: Understanding the basic principles of phonetics and phonology is fundamental to improving pronunciation. This involves learning the correct placement and movement of the articulators, such as the tongue, lips, and vocal cords, to produce accurate sounds.

2. Mimicry and Shadowing: One effective technique for accent reduction is mimicry. By imitating native speakers, learners can enhance their ability to reproduce sounds accurately. Shadowing, on the other hand, involves listening to a recording and simultaneously repeating what is being said. These techniques help develop muscle memory and improve pronunciation.

3. Recording and Listening: Recording your own voice while speaking allows you to analyze and identify areas where pronunciation needs improvement. By comparing your speech with that of native speakers, you can pinpoint specific sounds, stress patterns, or intonation that may require attention.

4. Minimal Pairs: Minimal pairs are words that differ by only one sound, such as "ship" and "sheep." Practicing minimal pairs helps learners identify and produce sounds that may not exist or differ in their native language. Regular practice with minimal pairs improves pronunciation accuracy.

5. Intonation and Rhythm: Paying attention to intonation, stress patterns, and rhythm is essential for clear communication. Understanding the melody of a language and using appropriate stress and intonation patterns enhances comprehension and reduces accent-related misunderstandings.

6. Speech Therapy: For those struggling with accent reduction, seeking professional help from a speech therapist can be highly beneficial. A speech therapist can provide personalized guidance, identify specific speech patterns that need improvement, and offer targeted exercises to address individual challenges.

Remember, accent reduction is a gradual process that requires consistent practice and patience. It is important to create a supportive environment and remain motivated throughout the journey. By implementing the techniques outlined in this subchapter, individuals can enhance their pronunciation skills, break down communication barriers, and achieve effective and confident communication in any language.

Embracing Your Unique Voice

Subchapter: Embracing Your Unique Voice

In the vast world of language education, it is crucial to acknowledge and celebrate the uniqueness of every individual's voice. Your voice is not just a tool for communication; it is an expression of your identity, culture, and personality. In this subchapter, we will explore the importance of embracing your unique voice and how it can enhance your pronunciation skills.

One of the fundamental principles of language education is to strive for clear and effective communication. However, this does not mean conforming to a standard accent or sounding like a native speaker. Each person brings their own background and experiences to the language learning journey, and this diversity should be celebrated.

Embracing your unique voice means accepting and valuing the way you express yourself in a foreign language. It recognizes that your pronunciation may differ from others, but it does not make it any less valid. Instead of striving for perfection, focus on clear and confident communication. Remember, the goal is to be understood rather than sounding like a native speaker.

By accepting your unique voice, you can develop a more authentic and personal connection with the language you are learning. Embrace the rhythms, intonations, and inflections that reflect your cultural background and linguistic roots. Your voice is a powerful tool that can bring a rich tapestry of diversity to your language skills.

Furthermore, embracing your unique voice allows you to develop a deeper understanding and appreciation for other accents and dialects. By celebrating your own voice, you become more open-minded and inclusive when interacting with people from different linguistic backgrounds. Language education becomes a journey of cultural exchange and mutual respect.

Perfecting your pronunciation is not about erasing your identity; it is about refining your skills while maintaining your authenticity. Practice and seek guidance to improve clarity, but never lose sight of the beauty and power of your unique voice.

In conclusion, embracing your unique voice is an essential aspect of language education. By valuing and celebrating your own voice, you enhance your pronunciation skills while maintaining your authenticity and cultural identity. Remember, communication is about understanding and being understood, not conforming to a standardized accent. Embrace the diversity of voices that language education brings, and let your unique voice shine through.

In the vast world of language education, one aspect that often goes overlooked is the importance of embracing your unique voice. Many learners become so preoccupied with perfecting their pronunciation that they forget the essence of communication lies in expressing oneself authentically. This subchapter aims to guide readers on the journey of discovering and embracing their distinctive voice, ultimately enhancing their language proficiency and overall communication skills.

When it comes to pronunciation, it is essential to remember that there is no single "correct" way to speak a language. Every language has numerous regional accents, dialects, and individual variations. These variations are what make language diverse and beautiful. By embracing your unique voice, you not only honor your cultural background but also bring an authentic touch to your communication.

To begin embracing your unique voice, it is crucial to develop self-awareness. Understand your natural tendencies, accent, and pronunciation patterns. This self-awareness will help you identify areas for improvement while staying true to your individuality. Embrace the sounds that come naturally to you, and learn to appreciate the unique qualities they bring to your speech.

Next, immerse yourself in the sounds and rhythms of the language you are learning. Listen to native speakers, watch movies or TV shows, and engage with the language through songs and podcasts. By exposing yourself to a variety of voices, you will expand your understanding of the language's nuances and develop a more diverse and adaptable pronunciation.

Another key aspect of embracing your unique voice is building confidence. Recognize that your voice is valuable and that you have something meaningful to contribute to conversations. Practice speaking aloud, even if it feels uncomfortable at first. Remember, the more you practice, the more confident you will become in utilizing your unique voice effectively.

Finally, seek feedback from native speakers or language teachers who can guide you through your pronunciation journey. They can identify areas where you may need improvement while ensuring that you maintain your unique voice. It is crucial to strike a balance between refining your pronunciation skills and preserving your individuality.

By embracing your unique voice, you will not only enhance your language proficiency but also develop a deeper connection with the language and its culture. Remember, language is a tool for communication and self-expression, and your unique voice adds richness and authenticity to the conversations you engage in. So, celebrate your individuality, embrace your unique voice, and let it shine through as you perfect your pronunciation and become a confident communicator in any language.

Achieving Clarity in Speech

In the vast world of language education, one aspect that often gets overlooked is the importance of achieving clarity in speech. Whether you are a non-native speaker seeking to improve your pronunciation or a native speaker looking to enhance your communication skills, mastering clarity in speech is pivotal. This subchapter aims to equip readers with practical tools and techniques to perfect their pronunciation and express themselves clearly, regardless of their linguistic background.

Understanding the significance of clarity in speech is crucial. Effective communication not only ensures that your message is understood but also helps you build rapport and convey your thoughts with confidence. To achieve this, the first step is awareness. By familiarizing yourself with the specific sounds and intonations of the language you are learning or refining, you can begin to identify areas for improvement.

The journey towards clarity in speech involves a combination of techniques and exercises. One such technique is phonetic transcription, which helps you break down words into individual sounds. By practicing the correct pronunciation of each sound, you can gradually eliminate any existing pronunciation errors. Additionally, mimicking native speakers through listening exercises and repetition can greatly aid in refining your pronunciation, as it allows you to internalize the natural rhythm and intonation of the language.

Furthermore, understanding the importance of stress and emphasis in speech is vital for clarity. Every language has its own set of rules regarding word stress, and familiarizing yourself with these patterns can significantly enhance your spoken communication. By correctly placing emphasis on the right syllables and words, you can convey your message with greater impact and clarity.

In addition to these techniques, this subchapter will explore the role of facial muscles and breath control in achieving clarity in speech. Through targeted exercises, readers will learn how to engage their articulatory organs effectively and harness the power of breath to support their pronunciation.

Perfecting Your Pronunciation: A Comprehensive Guide for Everyone offers a holistic approach to achieving clarity in speech. By combining techniques, exercises, and a deep understanding of the intricacies of language, readers will be equipped to express themselves with greater confidence and effectiveness. Whether you are a language learner or an educator seeking to enhance your teaching methods, this subchapter is an invaluable resource on your journey towards perfecting your pronunciation and achieving clarity in speech.

Clear and effective communication is essential in our everyday lives. Whether you are a student, a professional, or simply someone who enjoys conversing with others, having clarity in your speech can make a world of difference. In this subchapter, we will explore various techniques and exercises that will help you achieve clarity in your speech, enabling you to be understood more easily and express yourself with confidence.

1. Articulation: Proper articulation is key to clear speech. Pay attention to how you pronounce each sound and practice proper mouth positioning. Exercises such as tongue twisters can be incredibly helpful in improving your articulation skills.

2. Pronunciation: Correct pronunciation is vital for effective communication. Take the time to learn the pronunciation rules of your target language and practice them regularly. Listen to native speakers, imitate their sounds, and seek feedback from language teachers or native speakers to ensure that you are pronouncing words correctly.

3. Enunciation: Enunciation refers to the clarity with which you pronounce words and syllables. Speak slowly and enunciate each sound clearly, especially when speaking in a foreign language. This will help your listeners understand you better and avoid any confusion.

4. Stress and intonation: Pay attention to the stress and intonation patterns in sentences. Proper use of stress and intonation can significantly enhance the clarity and meaning of your speech. Practice reading aloud, focusing on emphasizing the correct words and using appropriate intonation for different types of sentences.

5. Breathing and voice projection: Good breath control and voice projection are crucial for clarity in speech. Practice deep breathing techniques to ensure you have enough air to support your voice. Project your voice by speaking from your diaphragm rather than your throat. This will help you speak louder and clearer without straining your vocal cords.

6. Practice active listening: Effective communication is a two-way street. Practice active listening skills by paying attention to how others speak. Observe their pronunciation, intonation, and articulation. By actively listening, you can learn from others and incorporate their techniques into your own speech.

Remember, achieving clarity in speech takes time and practice. Be patient with yourself and persistent in your efforts. Taking the time to focus on these techniques will not only improve your pronunciation but also boost your overall communication skills. Whether you are learning a new language or striving to perfect your pronunciation in your native tongue, the rewards of achieving clarity in speech are immense.

Chapter 11: Building Fluency and Confidence

Practicing Pronunciation Regularly

In the vast world of language education, mastering pronunciation is often seen as one of the most challenging aspects for learners of all levels. However, perfecting your pronunciation is not an impossible feat. With dedication and regular practice, anyone can improve their pronunciation skills and speak with clarity and confidence.

This subchapter aims to provide readers with practical tips and exercises to help them practice pronunciation regularly. By incorporating these techniques into your daily language learning routine, you will notice significant improvements in your ability to pronounce sounds accurately and communicate effectively.

First and foremost, it is essential to understand the importance of listening. By actively listening to native speakers, you train your ears to recognize the correct pronunciation of words and phrases. Engage with authentic audio materials, such as podcasts, music, or movies in your target language, and try to imitate the native speakers' intonation, stress, and rhythm. This immersive approach will help you internalize the sounds of the language and improve your overall pronunciation.

Next, focus on individual sounds. Each language has its unique set of phonemes, which can be challenging for non-native speakers to master. Dedicate time to practice the specific sounds that are difficult for you. Use online resources or language learning apps that provide audio examples and exercises for each sound. Regularly practicing these sounds will enable you to develop muscle memory and produce them more accurately.

Another effective way to practice pronunciation is through tongue twisters and minimal pairs. Tongue twisters are sentences or phrases that are challenging to articulate due to similar sounds or combinations. Recite them slowly and gradually increase your speed as you become more comfortable. Minimal pairs, on the other hand, are words that differ in only one sound, such as "ship" and "sheep." Practice distinguishing between these words to fine-tune your pronunciation skills.

Additionally, recording yourself while speaking in the target language can be a valuable tool for self-assessment. Listen to the recordings and compare them to native speakers' pronunciation. Identify areas where you need improvement and focus on those specific sounds or words during your practice sessions.

Lastly, join language exchange programs or conversation groups where you can interact with native speakers. Engaging in conversations will provide you with real-time feedback and help you identify any pronunciation errors. Native speakers can offer guidance and correct your mistakes, allowing you to refine your pronunciation further.

In conclusion, practicing pronunciation regularly is crucial for anyone looking to perfect their language skills. By incorporating active listening, focusing on individual sounds, using tongue twisters and minimal pairs, recording yourself, and engaging with native speakers, you will make significant strides in your pronunciation abilities.

Remember, consistent practice is the key to achieving clear and confident communication in any language.

In the journey of language learning, pronunciation plays a vital role in effective communication. Perfecting Your Pronunciation: A Comprehensive Guide for Everyone aims to provide valuable insights and practical techniques to help you improve your pronunciation skills. One key aspect emphasized in this book is the importance of practicing pronunciation regularly.

Whether you are a beginner or an advanced learner, consistent practice is crucial to achieve accurate pronunciation. Regular practice not only helps you develop muscle memory but also enhances your ability to produce sounds correctly. By incorporating pronunciation exercises into your daily routine, you can gradually refine your pronunciation skills and gain confidence in speaking the language.

To make the most of your practice sessions, it is essential to adopt a systematic approach. Start by identifying the specific sounds or phonemes that pose a challenge for you. Focus on those areas and dedicate time to practice them individually. This targeted practice will allow you to concentrate on improving the specific aspects that need attention, leading to noticeable progress over time.

Utilizing a variety of resources and techniques can also enhance your pronunciation practice. Audio materials, such as podcasts or language learning apps, can provide ample opportunities to listen to native speakers and imitate their pronunciation. You can also create your own audio recordings to compare and fine-tune your pronunciation. Additionally, practicing with a language partner or joining a conversation group can offer valuable feedback and create a supportive environment for improvement.

Incorporating pronunciation exercises into your daily routine will help you establish a habit of regular practice. Set aside dedicated time each day to focus solely on pronunciation. Be consistent and patient with yourself, as mastering pronunciation is a gradual process that requires time and effort. Celebrate small victories along the way to stay motivated and encouraged.

Remember, practicing pronunciation regularly is not only about correcting errors but also about developing a natural and confident speaking style. By dedicating time and effort to improve your pronunciation skills, you will not only enhance your overall language proficiency but also gain the ability to express yourself clearly and effectively.

Perfecting Your Pronunciation: A Comprehensive Guide for Everyone aims to empower language learners with the tools and knowledge necessary to improve their pronunciation. By embracing regular practice and utilizing the techniques presented in this book, you can embark on a journey towards achieving clear and accurate pronunciation, ultimately enhancing your language education and communication abilities.

Speaking with Native English Speakers

One of the most effective ways to perfect your pronunciation and improve your fluency in English is by engaging in conversations with native English speakers. This subchapter will provide you with valuable tips and strategies to make the most out of these interactions and enhance your language skills.

When speaking with native English speakers, it is essential to adopt a positive and open mindset. Don't be afraid to make mistakes or feel embarrassed about your accent. Remember that native speakers are generally understanding and supportive, and they can help you identify areas for improvement.

Take advantage of every opportunity to converse with native English speakers. Whether it's in a formal setting, such as language exchange programs or speaking clubs, or informal situations like social gatherings or community events, make an effort to engage in conversations. The more you practice, the more comfortable and confident you will become.

Active listening is a crucial aspect of speaking with native English speakers. Pay attention to their pronunciation, intonation, and rhythm. Observe how they use different expressions and idioms in context. By actively listening, you can start to mimic their speech patterns and incorporate them into your own language repertoire.

Don't hesitate to ask questions. Native speakers can provide valuable insights into the nuances of the language and help clarify any doubts you may have. They can also offer guidance on how to improve your pronunciation and suggest resources that have helped them in their language learning journey.

Additionally, consider using technology to your advantage. Record conversations with native speakers and listen to them later. This will allow you to focus on specific areas for improvement, such as stress, intonation, or vowel sounds. There are also various language learning apps and websites that connect language learners with native speakers for virtual conversations and language exchanges.

Finally, be patient and persistent. Perfecting pronunciation takes time and practice. Don't get discouraged if you encounter difficulties along the way. Embrace each interaction as an opportunity to learn and grow.

In conclusion, speaking with native English speakers is an invaluable tool for perfecting your pronunciation and enhancing your language skills. By adopting a positive mindset, actively listening, asking questions, utilizing technology, and remaining patient, you can make significant progress in your journey towards fluency. Embrace every opportunity to engage in conversations with native English speakers and watch as your pronunciation and confidence soar.

Engaging in conversations with native English speakers is an essential step towards perfecting your pronunciation and fluency in the language. Interacting with individuals who have grown up speaking English as their first language provides valuable opportunities to learn and improve your skills. In this subchapter, we will explore the benefits of speaking with native English speakers and provide practical tips to maximize your learning experience.

One of the advantages of conversing with native English speakers is the exposure to authentic pronunciation and intonation patterns. By listening to and imitating their speech, you can develop a more natural and native-like accent. Native speakers can also help you correct any mispronunciations or errors in your speech, guiding you towards better articulation and clarity.

Moreover, speaking with native English speakers enhances your understanding of the language's cultural nuances and idiomatic expressions. Language is deeply intertwined with culture, and by engaging in conversations with natives, you can gain insights into their way of thinking, their customs, and the context in which certain phrases or words are used. This cultural understanding will greatly enhance your communication skills and make you more confident in a variety of social and professional situations.

To make the most of your interactions with native English speakers, it is important to approach conversations with an open mind and a willingness to learn. Be proactive in seeking out opportunities to engage with native speakers, whether through language exchange programs, social gatherings, or online platforms. Don't be afraid to make mistakes or ask for clarification – native speakers are usually more than happy to help.

Additionally, practicing active listening is crucial when conversing with native English speakers. Pay attention to their pronunciation, intonation, and rhythm. Observe their body language and facial expressions to better understand the context and meaning behind their words. By actively listening, you can pick up on subtle nuances and improve your overall comprehension skills.

In conclusion, speaking with native English speakers is an invaluable part of perfecting your pronunciation and fluency. It provides you with exposure to authentic language use, cultural understanding, and opportunities for feedback and correction. Embrace these interactions as opportunities for growth and improvement, and you will undoubtedly see progress in your language skills. So, go ahead, seek out native English speakers, engage in conversations, and watch your pronunciation soar to new heights.

Engaging in Conversations and Discussions

In the realm of language education, one of the most crucial aspects of mastering any language is the ability to engage in conversations and discussions with confidence and fluency. This subchapter aims to equip readers from all walks of life with the necessary skills to perfect their pronunciation and effectively communicate their thoughts and ideas.

To engage in meaningful conversations, it is vital to pay attention to both verbal and non-verbal cues. Understanding the nuances of body language, facial expressions, and gestures can greatly enhance communication. This subchapter will delve into the importance of these non-verbal elements and how they can be utilized to convey messages more effectively.

Moreover, it is crucial to develop active listening skills to engage in fruitful discussions. Active listening involves not only hearing the words but also comprehending their meaning and context. Techniques such as paraphrasing, asking clarifying questions, and providing feedback are explored in detail to help readers become better listeners and participants in conversations.

Mastering pronunciation plays a pivotal role in engaging in conversations. This subchapter provides practical tips and exercises to improve pronunciation, focusing on vowel and consonant sounds, stress patterns, and intonation. By addressing common pronunciation challenges, readers will gain the confidence to express themselves clearly and be understood by others.

Furthermore, this subchapter will explore the importance of expanding one's vocabulary and utilizing appropriate expressions in different contexts. It delves into strategies for expanding vocabulary, such as reading extensively, practicing word associations, and learning collocations. It also emphasizes the significance of cultural sensitivity in language use, as it plays a crucial role in effective communication.

Lastly, this subchapter touches upon the art of persuasive speaking and debating. It provides readers with techniques to construct compelling arguments, present evidence, and counter opposing viewpoints. Through understanding rhetorical devices, logical reasoning, and persuasive language, readers will be equipped to engage in discussions and debates with confidence and eloquence.

Engaging in Conversations and Discussions is a vital subchapter for anyone seeking to perfect their pronunciation and excel in language education. By incorporating the techniques and strategies outlined in this subchapter, readers will become more effective communicators in various social and professional settings.

In the realm of language education, one crucial aspect that often goes overlooked is the ability to engage in meaningful conversations and discussions. While perfecting pronunciation is undoubtedly important, it is equally essential to develop the skills necessary to effectively communicate and express oneself through engaging in conversations. In this subchapter, we will delve into the art of conversation and provide you with valuable strategies to enhance your communication skills.

Engaging in conversations can be intimidating, especially for language learners. However, with the right mindset and practice, it can become an exciting and rewarding experience. The key is to embrace the opportunity to communicate with others, regardless of your level of proficiency. Remember, every conversation is an opportunity to improve your pronunciation, vocabulary, and overall language skills.

To begin, it is crucial to be an active listener. Pay attention to the person you are conversing with, and show genuine interest in what they have to say. Maintain eye contact, nod, and use appropriate body language to convey your engagement. This not only builds rapport but also allows you to pick up on the nuances of pronunciation and intonation.

Furthermore, it is important to take part in discussions and express your thoughts clearly. Don't be afraid to make mistakes, as they are an inevitable part of the learning process. Practice speaking confidently, and don't hesitate to ask for clarification if you don't understand something. Remember, the more you engage in conversations, the more comfortable you will become with the language.

Another effective strategy is to expand your vocabulary and knowledge base. Stay updated on current events, cultural trends, and various topics of interest. This will equip you with the necessary vocabulary and ideas to contribute meaningfully to discussions. Additionally, reading books, newspapers, and engaging in online forums can help you familiarize yourself with different writing styles, sentence structures, and expressions that can be incorporated into your conversations.

Lastly, embrace technology as a tool for enhancing your communication skills. Utilize language learning apps, join online language exchange platforms, or participate in virtual language meetups. These resources provide an opportunity to practice conversing with native speakers and fellow language enthusiasts, allowing you to receive immediate feedback and learn from others.

In conclusion, engaging in conversations and discussions is a vital component of language education. By actively listening, expressing your thoughts, expanding your vocabulary, and utilizing technology, you can enhance your communication skills and perfect your pronunciation. Embrace each conversation as an opportunity for growth and improvement, and soon you will find yourself confidently conversing in any language.

Overcoming Fear and Shyness

Introduction:
Fear and shyness can be significant barriers when it comes to perfecting your pronunciation. Whether you are learning a new language or aiming to improve your pronunciation in your native language, these emotions can hinder your progress. However, it is important to remember that fear and shyness are common and can be overcome with the right strategies and mindset. In this subchapter, we will explore effective techniques to help you conquer your fears and shyness, enabling you to improve your pronunciation with confidence.

Understanding Fear and Shyness:
Fear and shyness are natural human emotions. Fear often stems from the uncertainty of making mistakes or being judged, while shyness may arise from a lack of self-confidence or past negative experiences. Recognizing these emotions and their impact on your pronunciation journey is the first step towards overcoming them.

Building Confidence:
To overcome fear and shyness, it is crucial to build confidence in your abilities. Begin by setting realistic goals for your pronunciation improvement. Break down the process into smaller, achievable steps, celebrating each milestone along the way. Surround yourself with supportive individuals, such as language exchange partners or teachers, who can provide constructive feedback and encouragement.

Practicing in a Safe Environment:
Creating a safe environment for practice can greatly reduce fear and shyness. Find a comfortable space where you can freely experiment

with different sounds and pronunciations without the fear of judgment. Incorporate fun activities like tongue twisters or tongue exercises that aid in developing muscle memory and articulation.

Embracing   Mistakes:
Mistakes are an inevitable part of the learning process. Instead of being afraid of them, embrace them as opportunities for growth. Understand that making mistakes is an essential step towards improving your pronunciation. Learn from each error and view them as valuable lessons that will ultimately enhance your skills.

Visualization   and   Positive   Affirmations:
Visualizing success and using positive affirmations can be powerful tools in overcoming fear and shyness. Imagine yourself confidently speaking with impeccable pronunciation, and repeat positive statements to reinforce your belief in your abilities. These techniques can help rewire your mindset, replacing fear and shyness with positivity and self-assurance.

Conclusion:
Overcoming fear and shyness is essential for anyone seeking to perfect their pronunciation skills. By understanding the underlying causes of these emotions and implementing effective strategies, such as building confidence, practicing in a safe environment, embracing mistakes, and utilizing visualization and positive affirmations, you can conquer these barriers and unlock your full potential. Remember, perfecting your pronunciation is a journey, and with perseverance and the right mindset, you can achieve the desired results.

Introduction:
In the journey of perfecting your pronunciation, it is crucial to address the obstacles that may hinder your progress. Fear and shyness can significantly impact your ability to communicate effectively in a foreign language. This subchapter aims to empower individuals from all walks of life, interested in language education, with practical strategies to conquer fear and shyness.

Understanding   Fear   and   Shyness:
Fear and shyness often stem from a lack of confidence or past negative experiences. They can manifest as anxiety, nervousness, or self-doubt when speaking a foreign language. Recognizing and acknowledging these emotions is the first step towards overcoming them.

Building   Confidence:
Building confidence is key to conquering fear and shyness. Start by setting realistic goals and celebrating small victories along the way. Surround yourself with supportive people who encourage your language learning journey. Practice regularly and seek feedback from trusted individuals or language professionals to boost your confidence.

Mindset   Shift:
Adopting a positive mindset is crucial to overcoming fear and shyness. Embrace a growth mindset, understanding that mistakes are an inherent part of the learning process. Instead of fearing judgement, view each interaction as an opportunity to improve and grow. Remember, everyone makes mistakes, and it is through these errors that we learn and refine our pronunciation.

Immersion and Exposure: Immersing yourself in the language and culture can help alleviate fear and shyness. Engage in activities that expose you to native speakers, such as language exchange programs or joining conversation clubs. By surrounding yourself with the language, you will gradually become more comfortable with speaking and overcome any inhibitions.

Visualization and Positive Affirmations: Visualization and positive affirmations can be powerful tools in combating fear and shyness. Visualize yourself confidently speaking the language and achieving your language learning goals. Practice positive affirmations, repeating phrases such as "I am capable of speaking fluently" or "I embrace challenges and grow through them." These techniques can help rewire your mindset and build self-assurance.

Seeking Support: Remember, you are not alone in your language learning journey. Seek support from fellow language learners, language teachers, or online communities. Sharing experiences and challenges can provide valuable insights and encouragement. Additionally, consider seeking professional guidance from language coaches or therapists who specialize in language education.

Conclusion:
Overcoming fear and shyness is crucial in perfecting your pronunciation and achieving language fluency. By implementing the strategies outlined in this subchapter, individuals from all backgrounds can conquer their fears and confidently communicate in a foreign language. Embrace the journey, celebrate progress, and

remember that with dedication and perseverance, you can overcome any obstacle in your language learning path.

Celebrating Progress and Success

In the journey of perfecting your pronunciation, it is crucial to pause and acknowledge the progress you have made along the way. This subchapter, "Celebrating Progress and Success," aims to remind everyone engaged in language education that success is not only achieved through reaching the end goal but also through the small victories and milestones achieved throughout the process.

Learning a new language can be a challenging endeavor, and it is easy to get caught up in the pursuit of perfection. However, it is important to remember that progress is not always linear. There will be days when you feel like you're making tremendous strides, and others when it seems like you're standing still. It is during these moments that celebrating the progress you have made becomes even more crucial.

One way to celebrate success is by setting small, achievable goals. Break down your language learning journey into manageable steps and celebrate each time you accomplish one. Whether it's mastering a specific sound or successfully pronouncing a difficult word, these small victories should be acknowledged and celebrated. By doing so, you not only boost your motivation but also reinforce the belief that you are capable of achieving your larger goals.

Another important aspect of celebrating progress and success is acknowledging the effort you put into your language education. Learning a new language takes time, dedication, and perseverance. Recognize the hours you have spent practicing pronunciation, listening to native speakers, and engaging with the language in various ways. By acknowledging the effort, you give yourself credit for the hard work you have invested.

Furthermore, celebrating progress and success can be a communal experience. Share your accomplishments with others who are also on a language learning journey. Join language learning communities, participate in language exchange programs, or simply engage with fellow language learners online. By celebrating together, you create a supportive network that uplifts and motivates each other.

Remember, progress and success are not solely measured by achieving native-like pronunciation. Each step forward, no matter how small, is a testament to your dedication and resilience. Embrace the journey, celebrate your victories, and recognize the progress you have made. Perfecting Your Pronunciation is not just about reaching a destination; it's about the growth and transformation that occurs along the way.

Subchapter: Celebrating Progress and Success

In the journey of language education, it is essential to pause and acknowledge the progress and success we achieve along the way. Celebrating these milestones not only boosts our confidence but also motivates us to continue perfecting our pronunciation. This subchapter, "Celebrating Progress and Success," aims to highlight the importance of recognizing and celebrating our accomplishments in language learning.

Learning a new language can be a challenging endeavor, especially when it comes to mastering pronunciation. However, by focusing on continuous improvement and celebrating our progress, we can turn this journey into an enjoyable and fulfilling experience.

One of the key aspects of celebrating progress is setting achievable goals. By breaking down the learning process into smaller, attainable milestones, we can measure our progress more effectively. Whether it is correctly pronouncing a difficult sound or improving our intonation, each step forward deserves recognition. By acknowledging these achievements, we cultivate a positive mindset that fuels our motivation to keep learning and improving.

Furthermore, celebrating success can take various forms, depending on personal preferences. Some individuals find joy in sharing their accomplishments with others, while others prefer more personal rewards. Regardless of the method, the important thing is to acknowledge and appreciate our efforts.

Another aspect of celebrating progress and success is reflecting on the journey. Language education is not merely about reaching a destination; it is about the growth and development we experience along the way. By looking back at where we started and how far we have come, we gain a deeper appreciation for the progress we have made. This reflection helps us stay motivated, even during challenging times, by reminding us of our ability to overcome obstacles.

Lastly, celebrating progress and success should not be limited to individual achievements. Engaging in a supportive community of language learners can provide a platform for sharing accomplishments, seeking encouragement, and celebrating together. By surrounding ourselves with like-minded individuals who understand the struggles and victories of language education, we create a network that fosters growth and provides a space for mutual celebration.

In conclusion, "Celebrating Progress and Success" is a vital subchapter in the book "Perfecting Your Pronunciation: A Comprehensive Guide for Everyone." By recognizing and celebrating our progress, setting achievable goals, reflecting on the journey, and engaging with a supportive community, we can make language education an enriching and enjoyable experience for all. Let us celebrate the milestones along the way and embrace the joy of perfecting our pronunciation.

Chapter 12: Resources for Continued Learning

Online Pronunciation Tools and Apps

In this digital age, the accessibility and convenience of online tools and apps have revolutionized the way we approach language education. When it comes to perfecting your pronunciation, there is a wide array of online resources available at your fingertips. Whether you are a language learner, a teacher, or simply someone looking to improve their speaking skills, these tools and apps can be invaluable in your journey towards achieving flawless pronunciation.

One of the most popular online pronunciation tools is the use of interactive websites. These websites provide a platform for learners to practice their pronunciation skills through a variety of exercises. Users can listen to native speakers, record their own voice, and compare their pronunciation with the correct pronunciation. This immediate feedback is crucial in identifying and addressing any areas of weakness. Some websites even offer personalized pronunciation lessons based on individual needs, making the learning experience even more tailored and effective.

In addition to interactive websites, pronunciation apps have also gained popularity in recent years. These apps offer a more portable and on-the-go solution for language learners. With features such as voice recognition technology, these apps can analyze and provide feedback on your pronunciation in real-time. They often come with engaging games and exercises to make the learning process enjoyable and interactive. Furthermore, many pronunciation apps have extensive databases of words and phrases, allowing users to practice pronouncing a wide range of vocabulary.

Another useful aspect of online pronunciation tools and apps is the ability to connect with native speakers and language experts from around the world. Some platforms provide forums or chat rooms where learners can engage in conversations with these language experts. This not only helps improve pronunciation but also enhances overall language proficiency through exposure to authentic and natural speech.

Regardless of your proficiency level or language of interest, online pronunciation tools and apps offer a convenient and effective way to enhance your pronunciation skills. They provide a flexible learning experience, allowing you to practice whenever and wherever you want. Whether you are looking to improve your accent, reduce your accent, or simply refine your pronunciation, these tools can be a valuable addition to your language learning journey.

In conclusion, the advent of online pronunciation tools and apps has transformed the way we approach language education. With their interactive exercises, personalized lessons, real-time feedback, and opportunities for interaction with native speakers, these tools have made perfecting your pronunciation more accessible and enjoyable than ever before. So why wait? Start exploring these online resources today and unlock your full potential in pronunciation mastery.

In today's digital age, language education has become more accessible than ever before, thanks to the advent of online pronunciation tools and apps. These innovative resources are designed to help learners of all levels perfect their pronunciation skills in a convenient and interactive manner. By leveraging the power of technology, these tools provide a comprehensive guide for everyone interested in improving their pronunciation abilities.

One of the key advantages of online pronunciation tools and apps is their flexibility and convenience. Learners no longer need to attend physical classes or hire personal tutors to work on their pronunciation. With just a few clicks, anyone can access a wide range of pronunciation exercises, lessons, and activities from the comfort of their own home or on the go. This accessibility makes it possible for busy individuals to incorporate pronunciation practice into their daily routines, regardless of their schedules.

Moreover, these tools cater to learners of different proficiency levels, allowing everyone to find resources that suit their needs. Whether you are a beginner just starting your language-learning journey or an advanced speaker striving to fine-tune your accent, there are tools and apps available that offer targeted exercises and lessons to help you achieve your goals. From practicing individual sounds to mastering complex phonetic patterns, these resources cover a wide range of pronunciation challenges.

Online pronunciation tools and apps also foster interactivity and engagement, making learning a fun and immersive experience. Many platforms employ gamification techniques, turning pronunciation practice into an exciting game. Users can compete with friends, earn points, and unlock achievements as they progress, creating a sense of accomplishment and motivation to continue improving. Additionally, some tools provide real-time feedback, allowing learners to instantly correct their pronunciation errors and develop more accurate speech patterns.

In conclusion, online pronunciation tools and apps have revolutionized language education by providing accessible, comprehensive, and interactive resources for learners of all levels. Whether you are a student, a professional, or simply someone interested in improving your pronunciation, these tools offer a convenient and effective way to perfect your skills. Embrace the power of technology, and embark on a journey towards flawless pronunciation with the help of these invaluable resources.

Pronunciation Courses and Workshops

In today's globalized world, effective communication is paramount. Whether you are a language learner, a teacher, or someone simply interested in perfecting your pronunciation, this subchapter on "Pronunciation Courses and Workshops" will provide you with valuable insights and guidance.

Language Education has witnessed a surge in demand for pronunciation courses and workshops as learners recognize the importance of clear and accurate pronunciation in achieving fluency and confidence in speech. These courses and workshops are designed to cater to the diverse needs of individuals seeking to improve their pronunciation skills.

Pronunciation courses typically offer a systematic approach to mastering the sounds, intonation, and stress patterns of a particular language. They often employ various techniques and tools, such as phonetic exercises, audio recordings, and interactive activities to enhance learners' understanding and production of sounds. These courses usually have experienced instructors who provide personalized feedback and guidance to help learners overcome specific pronunciation challenges.

Workshops, on the other hand, are intensive and interactive sessions that offer targeted training on specific aspects of pronunciation. They may focus on areas like vowel and consonant sounds, rhythm and stress patterns, or even pronunciation in specific contexts like business or academic settings. Workshops often include group activities, role plays, and real-life simulations, allowing participants to practice their pronunciation skills in a supportive environment.

The benefits of attending pronunciation courses and workshops are numerous. Improved pronunciation not only enhances your ability to be understood by others, but it also boosts your confidence in expressing yourself fluently. Moreover, it can positively impact your overall language proficiency, as accurate pronunciation facilitates better listening comprehension and oral communication.

Whether you are a language learner aiming to achieve native-like pronunciation or a teacher seeking to enhance your pedagogical skills, pronunciation courses and workshops are invaluable resources. They provide a structured and focused approach to pronunciation training, ensuring that learners receive proper guidance and support throughout their journey.

In conclusion, pronunciation courses and workshops are essential components of language education. They offer learners the opportunity to refine their pronunciation skills, enabling them to communicate effectively and confidently in their target language. By investing in these courses and workshops, individuals can unlock the full potential of their linguistic abilities and become proficient and articulate communicators.

Language Education plays a vital role in our globalized world, where effective communication is key. One crucial aspect of language learning is pronunciation. A strong and accurate pronunciation not only enhances our ability to be understood but also boosts our confidence when speaking in a foreign language. If you have ever struggled with pronunciation or wish to perfect your skills, Pronunciation Courses and Workshops are the answer.

Pronunciation Courses and Workshops are designed to cater to the needs of individuals from all walks of life, regardless of their language proficiency level. Whether you are a beginner or an advanced learner, these courses provide a comprehensive guide to help you perfect your pronunciation.

These courses typically cover a wide range of topics, including phonetics, phonology, intonation, stress patterns, and articulation. They focus on both individual sounds and connected speech, enabling learners to understand and produce accurate sounds in real-life situations. Through interactive activities and exercises, these courses provide hands-on practice, allowing learners to apply their knowledge immediately.

Workshops are often conducted by experienced language educators who specialize in phonetics and pronunciation. They employ various teaching methods and techniques to meet the diverse learning needs of participants. These may include group activities, role-plays, tongue twisters, and audiovisual materials. The workshops not only provide a conducive learning environment but also foster a sense of community among participants, creating a supportive and collaborative atmosphere.

Moreover, Pronunciation Courses and Workshops employ a learner-centered approach, tailoring the content and pace to suit the needs of individual learners. Whether you want to focus on a specific sound or improve your overall pronunciation skills, these courses offer a personalized learning experience.

In addition to language learners, these courses are also beneficial for language teachers who wish to enhance their teaching skills. By attending Pronunciation Courses and Workshops, educators can gain valuable insights and strategies to effectively teach pronunciation to their students. This knowledge can then be applied in classrooms, making language learning a more enriching and enjoyable experience for both teachers and students.

In conclusion, Pronunciation Courses and Workshops offer a comprehensive guide for individuals seeking to perfect their pronunciation skills. Whether you are a language learner or a language teacher, these courses provide valuable insights and practical techniques to enhance pronunciation. By investing in Pronunciation Courses and Workshops, you can gain the confidence and skills necessary to communicate effectively in any language. So, take the first step towards perfecting your pronunciation and enroll in a Pronunciation Course or Workshop today!

Pronunciation Communities and Forums

In the world of language education, the journey towards perfecting pronunciation can sometimes feel like a solitary pursuit. However, thanks to the rise of online communities and forums, learners from all walks of life can now come together to support and learn from one another. These virtual spaces have become a valuable resource for individuals seeking to improve their pronunciation skills, providing a platform for sharing experiences, asking questions, and receiving feedback.

One of the main benefits of joining pronunciation communities and forums is the opportunity for interaction with a diverse range of language learners and experts. Regardless of your native language or target language, these communities bring together individuals who share a common goal: achieving better pronunciation. Through engaging in discussions, learners can gain insights into different techniques, tips, and exercises that have been successful for others. Additionally, these platforms allow for the exchange of cultural knowledge and understanding, fostering a sense of global community.

For learners who prefer a more structured approach, many forums offer pronunciation challenges and activities. These challenges often involve recording and sharing audio clips, allowing participants to receive constructive feedback from native speakers or experienced learners. This personalized feedback can be invaluable in identifying specific areas of improvement and providing guidance on how to overcome common pronunciation difficulties.

Moreover, pronunciation communities and forums are a treasure trove of resources. Members often share links to helpful websites, videos, and apps that offer targeted practice exercises, phonetic charts, and pronunciation guides. These resources, curated by fellow learners and experts, can save time and effort in searching for reliable materials elsewhere. Additionally, many communities organize virtual events, such as webinars or workshops, conducted by language professionals. These events provide a unique opportunity to learn directly from experts in the field, ensuring that learners receive accurate and up-to-date information.

In conclusion, pronunciation communities and forums play a crucial role in language education, offering a supportive and interactive space for learners to improve their pronunciation skills. These virtual platforms provide opportunities for learners to connect with others, share experiences, and receive personalized feedback. Furthermore, they offer access to a wealth of resources and expert knowledge, contributing to a comprehensive learning experience. By actively participating in these communities, learners can enhance their pronunciation abilities and feel motivated on their language learning journey.

In today's interconnected world, language learning has become more accessible than ever before. With the rise of the internet, learners can now connect with others from around the globe who share their passion for mastering pronunciation. Pronunciation communities and forums have emerged as valuable resources for language education, offering learners a platform to interact, practice, and perfect their pronunciation skills.

These online communities bring together individuals from diverse linguistic backgrounds, creating a rich and dynamic environment for language learning. Whether you are a beginner or an advanced learner, these communities provide a supportive space to ask questions, exchange feedback, and receive guidance from experienced speakers and experts. By actively participating in these forums, learners can gain valuable insights into the specific challenges they may face based on their native language and receive targeted advice to overcome them.

One of the key advantages of joining pronunciation communities and forums is the opportunity to engage in conversation practice. By interacting with native speakers and other language learners, individuals can fine-tune their pronunciation skills by imitating and receiving feedback on their speech. These communities often provide audio and video resources, allowing learners to compare their pronunciation with that of native speakers or experienced learners. This immersive experience is essential for developing a natural and authentic accent.

Moreover, these communities are also valuable sources of learning materials and resources. Members often share tips, techniques, and exercises that have proven effective in their own language journeys. They may recommend pronunciation apps, online courses, or language learning websites that have helped them improve their pronunciation. By leveraging the collective knowledge and experience of these communities, learners can access a wide range of resources to support their pronunciation practice.

Additionally, pronunciation communities and forums foster a sense of belonging and camaraderie among learners. The shared goal of perfecting pronunciation creates a supportive and motivating environment. Learners can celebrate their progress, share their achievements, and find inspiration in the successes of others. This sense of community can alleviate the isolation that some language learners may feel and provide the encouragement needed to persevere in their pronunciation journey.

In conclusion, pronunciation communities and forums offer a treasure trove of resources and support for language learners. Accessible to individuals of all proficiency levels, these platforms provide a space for learners to practice, receive feedback, and connect with others who share their passion for perfecting pronunciation. By actively engaging in these communities, learners can enhance their pronunciation skills, access valuable learning materials, and find a supportive network that empowers them to achieve their language goals.

Recommended Books and Literature

In the realm of language education, books and literature play a pivotal role in perfecting pronunciation skills and overall language proficiency. Whether you are a language learner or an educator, immersing yourself in the right resources can significantly enhance your pronunciation abilities. This subchapter aims to provide a comprehensive list of recommended books and literature that cater to individuals in the field of language education.

1. "The Phonetics of English and Dutch" by Beverley Collins and Inger M. Mees: This book offers a detailed analysis of the sounds and phonetics of English and Dutch. It delves into the intricacies of pronunciation, providing practical exercises and explanations to help learners grasp the nuances of these languages.

2. "English Pronunciation in Use" by Mark Hancock: This highly acclaimed book provides a systematic approach to mastering English pronunciation. It covers various aspects, such as individual sounds, stress, rhythm, intonation, and connected speech. With its interactive exercises and audio resources, learners can practice and refine their pronunciation skills.

3. "Accent Reduction For Professionals" by Susan Cameron: Geared towards individuals aiming to improve their pronunciation for professional purposes, this book offers practical strategies and exercises. It focuses on reducing accents that may hinder effective communication in the workplace, enabling learners to speak with clarity and confidence.

4. "Pronunciation Pairs" by Ann Baker: This resourceful book is designed for classroom use and self-study. It provides a wide range of activities, including tongue twisters, minimal pair exercises, and intonation drills. Through its comprehensive approach, learners can enhance their pronunciation skills in an engaging and interactive manner.

5. "The Cambridge Guide to English Pronunciation" by Peter Roach: As a comprehensive reference, this book covers pronunciation variations in English worldwide. It explores regional accents, intonation patterns, and common pronunciation difficulties faced by non-native speakers. With its clear explanations and audio examples, it serves as an invaluable tool for both learners and educators.

Additionally, immersing yourself in literature written in the target language can greatly contribute to improving pronunciation. Classic novels, contemporary literature, and even poetry can expose learners to the natural rhythm, intonation, and pronunciation patterns of the language. Reading aloud and listening to audiobooks can aid in internalizing these linguistic elements and refining pronunciation skills.

In conclusion, the recommended books and literature listed above provide a solid foundation for perfecting pronunciation and overall language proficiency. Whether you are a language learner or an educator, incorporating these resources into your language education journey can significantly enhance your pronunciation abilities and contribute to effective communication.

In the journey of perfecting your pronunciation, immersing yourself in the world of books and literature can offer invaluable benefits. Whether you are a language enthusiast looking to enhance your language skills or a teacher seeking effective resources for your students, this subchapter presents a collection of recommended books and literature to aid you on your pronunciation journey.

1. "The Pronunciation Book" by Adam Brown: This comprehensive guide is a must-have for anyone looking to improve their pronunciation skills. It covers a wide range of topics, from phonetics and phonology to intonation and stress patterns.

2. "Sounds of Language: An Introduction to Phonetics" by Henry Rogers: This book delves deep into the science of speech sounds, providing a solid foundation in phonetics. It offers exercises and activities that help learners grasp the intricacies of pronunciation.

3. "Pronunciation Pairs" by Ann Baker and Sharon Goldstein: This practical guide is ideal for language learners at any level. It focuses on minimal pairs, helping learners distinguish between similar sounds that often cause confusion.

4. "English Pronunciation in Use" by Mark Hancock: This self-study book is perfect for learners of English as a second language. It covers key pronunciation points, such as individual sounds, word stress, and connected speech, with interactive exercises and audio CDs.

5. "The Poetry of Robert Frost: Collected Poems" by Robert Frost: Exploring poetry can be an enjoyable way to enhance your pronunciation skills. Robert Frost's collection offers a rich variety of poems that require careful attention to rhythm, stress, and intonation.

6. "The Great Gatsby" by F. Scott Fitzgerald: Reading aloud passages from this classic American novel allows learners to practice their pronunciation, rhythm, and intonation, as they immerse themselves in the captivating story of Jay Gatsby.

7. "The Elements of Eloquence: How to Turn the Perfect English Phrase" by Mark Forsyth: This book explores the art of rhetoric and offers insights into the power of language. It provides examples of eloquent phrases and techniques that can inspire learners to improve their own pronunciation skills.

Remember, these recommended books and literature serve as valuable resources, but hands-on practice and interaction with native speakers remain crucial for achieving mastery in pronunciation. So, dive into these books, practice regularly, and witness your pronunciation skills soar to new heights.

Creating a Personalized Learning Plan

In the world of language education, one size does not fit all. Each individual has unique strengths, weaknesses, and learning styles. That's why it is essential to create a personalized learning plan to perfect your pronunciation. This subchapter will guide you on how to tailor your language learning journey to your specific needs, ensuring maximum success and efficiency.

The first step in creating a personalized learning plan is self-assessment. Take the time to evaluate your current pronunciation skills and identify areas that require improvement. Are you struggling with specific sounds, intonation patterns, or rhythm? Understanding your weaknesses will help you focus your efforts and resources on the areas that need the most attention.

Once you have identified your specific needs, it's time to set specific goals. Do you want to reduce your accent, speak more fluently, or sound more natural? Setting clear and attainable goals will help you stay motivated and measure your progress along the way. Remember to break down your goals into smaller, manageable tasks to make the learning process more achievable and less overwhelming.

Next, explore various resources and tools that align with your learning style. Some individuals prefer visual aids, while others thrive in interactive environments. Consider utilizing online courses, pronunciation apps, language exchange platforms, or even hiring a private tutor. Experiment with different methods and find the ones that resonate with you the most. Remember, a personalized learning plan means finding what works best for you.

Consistency is key when it comes to perfecting your pronunciation. Dedicate a specific amount of time each day or week to practice. Create a schedule that fits into your daily routine, ensuring that you have enough time to focus on your language learning goals. Make use of the resources available to you, such as audio exercises, tongue twisters, or even recording your voice to track your progress.

Lastly, embrace the power of feedback. Seek opportunities to practice speaking with native speakers or language experts who can provide constructive criticism. Join language exchange groups, attend conversation clubs, or enroll in pronunciation workshops. Feedback allows you to fine-tune your pronunciation and gain confidence in your speaking abilities.

Remember, creating a personalized learning plan is about tailoring your language education to your unique needs and goals. By assessing your skills, setting specific objectives, utilizing resources that suit your learning style, remaining consistent, and seeking feedback, you will be well on your way to perfecting your pronunciation and becoming a confident communicator in any language.

In the realm of language education, one of the keys to achieving proficiency and fluency is developing a personalized learning plan. Each individual has unique strengths, weaknesses, and learning styles, which is why a one-size-fits-all approach to language learning can often be ineffective. By tailoring your learning journey to fit your specific needs, goals, and preferences, you can maximize your progress and perfect your pronunciation.

The first step in creating a personalized learning plan is self-assessment. Take the time to identify your strengths and weaknesses in pronunciation. Are there specific sounds or phonetic patterns that you struggle with? Do you have difficulty with certain intonation or stress patterns? By pinpointing these areas, you can focus your efforts on improving them.

Next, set clear and achievable goals. Do you want to improve your overall pronunciation or focus on specific aspects? Are you aiming for native-like fluency or just aiming to be easily understood? Define your goals and break them down into smaller, manageable steps. This will help you stay motivated and track your progress along the way.

Once you have your objectives in place, it's time to explore different learning resources and techniques. There are numerous options available, such as online courses, pronunciation apps, language exchange programs, or working with a language tutor. Experiment with various methods and find what works best for you. Some individuals may thrive in a structured classroom environment, while others prefer self-paced learning or one-on-one instruction.

In addition to formal learning resources, don't underestimate the power of immersion and practice. Surround yourself with the language as much as possible. Listen to native speakers, watch movies or TV shows in the target language, and engage in conversations with native speakers whenever you can. This will expose you to authentic pronunciation models and provide invaluable opportunities to practice and refine your own pronunciation skills.

Lastly, be consistent and persistent in your efforts. Learning a language, especially perfecting your pronunciation, takes time and dedication. Set aside regular study sessions, practice daily, and remain committed to your personalized learning plan. Remember that progress may not always be linear, and setbacks are a natural part of the learning process. Stay positive, keep pushing forward, and celebrate each milestone you achieve along the way.

In conclusion, creating a personalized learning plan is essential for anyone embarking on a journey to perfect their pronunciation. By assessing your strengths and weaknesses, setting clear goals, exploring different learning resources, immersing yourself in the language, and remaining consistent, you can make significant strides in your language education. Remember, everyone's learning journey is unique, and by tailoring your plan to suit your individual needs, you can unleash your full potential and achieve pronunciation excellence.

Chapter 13: Conclusion

Recap of Key Concepts

Throughout this comprehensive guide on perfecting your pronunciation, we have covered a wide range of key concepts that are essential for anyone seeking to improve their language skills. Whether you are a language learner, a teacher, or simply someone interested in enhancing your pronunciation abilities, this subchapter will serve as a helpful recap of the main ideas discussed in this book.

One of the fundamental concepts we explored is the importance of understanding the International Phonetic Alphabet (IPA). By familiarizing yourself with the IPA symbols, you can accurately represent and reproduce the sounds of different languages. We delved into the various IPA symbols for vowels and consonants, providing clear explanations and examples to help you grasp their pronunciation.

Another key concept we highlighted is the significance of stress and intonation in spoken language. We discussed the role of stress in word syllables and its impact on meaning and communication. Additionally, we explored the importance of intonation in conveying emotions, attitudes, and rhetorical functions. By mastering stress and intonation patterns, you can greatly enhance your overall pronunciation skills.

We also touched upon the concept of connected speech, which refers to the way words and sounds blend together in natural spoken language. We examined phenomena such as assimilation, elision, and linking, offering practical tips and exercises to help you navigate these aspects of connected speech effectively.

Furthermore, we emphasized the significance of word and sentence stress in English pronunciation. By correctly emphasizing certain syllables or words in a sentence, you can convey important information and improve your overall intelligibility.

Lastly, we provided guidance on how to practice and improve your pronunciation skills. We discussed the benefits of using technology, such as language learning apps and online resources, as well as the importance of listening to native speakers and imitating their pronunciation. We also highlighted the value of receiving feedback from others, whether through language exchange partners, teachers, or pronunciation coaches.

In conclusion, this subchapter serves as a helpful recap of the key concepts covered in this book on perfecting your pronunciation. By understanding and practicing the International Phonetic Alphabet, stress and intonation patterns, connected speech, and word and sentence stress, you can make significant strides in improving your pronunciation skills. Remember to embrace technology, seek feedback, and dedicate regular practice sessions to perfect your pronunciation and enhance your language skills.

In this subchapter, we will go over the essential concepts discussed throughout this book, "Perfecting Your Pronunciation: A Comprehensive Guide for Everyone." Whether you are a language learner, a teacher, or simply someone interested in improving your pronunciation skills, this recap will help reinforce the key ideas and techniques covered in the previous chapters.

One of the fundamental concepts emphasized in this book is the importance of phonetics. Understanding the sounds of a language is crucial for accurate pronunciation. We explored the International Phonetic Alphabet (IPA), which provides a standardized way to represent sounds from different languages. By familiarizing yourself with the IPA symbols, you can easily identify and reproduce the correct sounds when learning a new language.

Another vital concept discussed is the distinction between vowels and consonants. Vowels are the building blocks of any language and mastering their pronunciation is crucial. We delved into the different vowel sounds, vowel length, and their placement within the mouth. By practicing these vowel sounds, you can significantly improve your pronunciation and intelligibility.

Consonants, on the other hand, add clarity and precision to speech. We explored various types of consonants, including plosives, fricatives, nasals, and approximants. Understanding how to produce these sounds correctly and efficiently is essential for clear communication.

Stress and intonation are two concepts that greatly impact how we are perceived when speaking a language. We discussed the importance of word stress and sentence stress, as well as the melody of speech. By mastering stress and intonation patterns, you can sound more natural and convey the intended meaning effectively.

Throughout the book, we also stressed the significance of practice. Perfecting your pronunciation requires consistent effort and repetition. We provided various exercises and activities to reinforce the concepts discussed, such as tongue twisters, minimal pairs, and listening exercises. By incorporating these activities into your language learning routine, you can make significant progress in your pronunciation skills.

In conclusion, this subchapter serves as a recap of the key concepts covered in "Perfecting Your Pronunciation: A Comprehensive Guide for Everyone." By understanding phonetics, vowels, consonants, stress, intonation, and the importance of practice, you can enhance your pronunciation skills and become a more confident speaker. Whether you are a language learner or a teacher in the field of language education, these concepts are crucial for effective communication in any language.

Reflecting on Your Pronunciation Journey

The journey to perfecting your pronunciation is an ongoing process that requires patience, dedication, and self-reflection. In this subchapter, we will delve into the importance of reflecting on your pronunciation journey and how it can contribute to your overall language education.

Pronunciation is a fundamental aspect of language learning, as it directly impacts your ability to communicate effectively and be understood by others. Reflecting on your pronunciation journey allows you to assess your progress, identify areas for improvement, and develop strategies to achieve your goals.

One of the first steps in reflecting on your pronunciation journey is to evaluate your current level of proficiency. Take the time to listen to yourself speaking in the target language, record your voice, and compare it to native speakers or audio resources. Pay attention to specific sounds, stress patterns, and intonation. This self-assessment will give you a clearer understanding of your strengths and weaknesses.

Once you have identified areas for improvement, it is essential to set realistic goals. Reflect on what you want to achieve in terms of pronunciation and break it down into manageable steps. This could include focusing on specific sounds or practicing certain tongue positions. By setting clear objectives, you can measure your progress and stay motivated on your pronunciation journey.

Regular practice is crucial in perfecting your pronunciation. Reflect on your daily routine and identify opportunities to incorporate pronunciation exercises. It could be during your commute, while doing household chores, or even during breaks at work. Consistency is key, so make a habit of practicing regularly and incorporating pronunciation exercises into your language education routine.

Reflecting on your pronunciation journey also involves seeking feedback from others. Engage in conversations with native speakers, language tutors, or join language exchange groups. Their feedback and guidance will help you identify areas that need improvement and provide insights into specific pronunciation challenges.

Remember to celebrate your successes along the way. Reflect on how far you have come and acknowledge the progress you have made. Language learning is a continuous journey, and every step forward is worth celebrating.

By reflecting on your pronunciation journey, you will gain a deeper understanding of your strengths and weaknesses, set realistic goals, practice regularly, seek feedback, and celebrate your progress. This subchapter aims to empower everyone in their language education journey by providing tools and techniques to perfect their pronunciation skills.

In the realm of language education, mastering pronunciation is often considered one of the most challenging aspects of learning a new language. It requires dedication, practice, and a keen ear to accurately capture the nuances and sounds of a foreign tongue. However, the journey towards perfecting your pronunciation is not only about achieving flawless speech but also about embracing the beauty of diversity and cultural understanding. In this subchapter, we will reflect on your pronunciation journey and explore the transformative power it holds for everyone.

Learning a new language can be a daunting task, and it is natural to feel frustrated or discouraged along the way. However, take a moment to reflect on how far you have come. Celebrate the progress you have made and the effort you have put into refining your pronunciation skills. Remember that every pronunciation hurdle you overcome is a stepping stone towards better communication and cultural exchange.

Reflecting on your pronunciation journey allows you to appreciate the diversity of languages and cultures. Each language has its unique set of sounds, intonations, and rhythms that shape its identity. By immersing yourself in the journey of perfecting your pronunciation, you open yourself up to a world of new experiences and perspectives. You gain a deeper understanding of different cultures and the way people communicate, fostering empathy and connection with others.

Moreover, reflecting on your pronunciation journey enables you to become a better communicator. As you refine your pronunciation skills, you become more confident in expressing yourself in the target language. This newfound confidence extends beyond pronunciation and positively impacts your overall language fluency. It empowers you to engage in meaningful conversations, build relationships, and navigate different social and professional settings with ease.

In this subchapter, we will explore techniques and exercises to help you reflect on your pronunciation journey. We will delve into the importance of self-awareness, embracing mistakes as opportunities for growth, and seeking feedback from native speakers or language instructors. By actively engaging in reflective practices, you can identify areas for improvement, set realistic goals, and develop effective strategies to enhance your pronunciation skills continuously.

Remember, perfecting your pronunciation is a lifelong journey, and even native speakers are constantly refining their skills. Embrace the process, be patient with yourself, and celebrate every milestone along the way. Your pronunciation journey is not only about achieving linguistic proficiency but also about fostering cross-cultural understanding, personal growth, and enriching connections with others.

Embracing Lifelong Learning

In today's fast-paced and ever-changing world, the importance of lifelong learning cannot be overstated. Whether you are a student, professional, or simply someone interested in language education, the concept of continuously improving your skills and knowledge is crucial for personal and professional growth. This subchapter will delve into the significance of embracing lifelong learning in the context of language education and provide practical tips on how to make it a part of your daily life.

Language education is not limited to formal classroom settings or textbooks. It extends far beyond that, encompassing a wide range of resources and opportunities. Embracing lifelong learning means acknowledging that language is a living entity, constantly evolving and adapting. It requires an open mind and a willingness to explore new methods and approaches to language learning.

One key aspect of lifelong learning is the ability to adapt to new technologies and tools. With the advent of technology, learning a language has become more accessible and convenient than ever before. Online platforms, mobile applications, and language learning websites offer interactive and engaging resources that can enhance your language skills. Embracing these tools and incorporating them into your learning routine can significantly accelerate your progress.

Another crucial element of lifelong learning is the willingness to step out of your comfort zone. Language education offers ample opportunities for immersion, whether it be through cultural exchanges, language exchange programs, or even traveling to a country where the language is spoken. Embracing these experiences not only allows you to practice your language skills in real-life situations but also exposes you to different cultures and perspectives, enriching your overall understanding of the language.

Additionally, lifelong learning requires a proactive approach. Setting goals, creating a study plan, and dedicating time to language learning on a regular basis are essential practices. By breaking down your language learning journey into smaller, manageable tasks, you can maintain a consistent and sustainable learning routine.

In conclusion, embracing lifelong learning in the context of language education is a mindset that fosters personal and professional growth. By being open to new technologies, stepping out of your comfort zone, and adopting a proactive approach, you can enhance your language skills, gain cultural insights, and expand your horizons. Remember, language learning is a lifelong journey, and with the right mindset, you can perfect your pronunciation and become a confident communicator in any language.

In today's fast-paced world, the importance of lifelong learning cannot be overstated. The desire to continuously improve oneself and acquire new knowledge and skills is essential, especially in the field of language education. Whether you are a student, a professional, or simply someone interested in perfecting your pronunciation, embracing lifelong learning will not only enhance your language proficiency but also enrich your personal and professional growth.

The journey of mastering pronunciation is a lifelong process that requires dedication, practice, and a willingness to learn. As language education evolves, new techniques and tools emerge, making it crucial for language learners to adapt and stay up to date with the latest advancements. Embracing lifelong learning means nurturing a growth mindset, where challenges are seen as opportunities for improvement, and mistakes are viewed as stepping stones to success.

One of the key benefits of lifelong learning is the ability to broaden your horizons. By actively seeking new learning opportunities, you expose yourself to different perspectives, cultures, and languages. This not only enhances your understanding of the world but also allows you to communicate effectively and connect with people from diverse backgrounds. Lifelong learning empowers you to become a global citizen, opening doors to new friendships, career opportunities, and personal growth.

Moreover, the process of lifelong learning fosters resilience and adaptability. In the ever-changing landscape of language education, it is crucial to be open to new methodologies, theories, and techniques. By embracing lifelong learning, you develop the ability to adapt to new teaching strategies, incorporate technology into your learning journey, and effectively navigate the challenges that come your way. This adaptability not only enhances your language proficiency but also equips you with transferrable skills that are highly valued in today's job market.

Furthermore, embracing lifelong learning keeps your mind active and engaged. As you continue to seek new knowledge and skills, you stimulate your brain and prevent cognitive decline. Studies have shown that lifelong learning can improve memory, critical thinking, and problem-solving abilities. By regularly challenging yourself to learn and perfect your pronunciation, you are investing in your cognitive health and overall well-being.

In conclusion, embracing lifelong learning is not just a choice, but a necessity in the field of language education. It equips you with the tools to constantly improve your pronunciation skills, expand your horizons, foster adaptability, and keep your mind active. By embracing lifelong learning, you embark on a fulfilling journey of personal and professional growth, enabling you to communicate effectively, connect with others, and thrive in an ever-evolving world. So, seize the opportunity, unlock your potential, and embrace the limitless possibilities that lifelong learning has to offer.

Final Words of Encouragement

The index is an essential tool for any language learner seeking to perfect their pronunciation. This comprehensive guide, "Perfecting Your Pronunciation: A Comprehensive Guide for Everyone," recognizes the importance of organizing information in a way that is accessible and easy to navigate. In this subchapter, we will explore how the index can assist language learners in their quest for improved pronunciation.

The index serves as a roadmap to the content within this book, allowing readers to quickly locate specific topics, exercises, and techniques related to pronunciation. It is designed to cater to the needs of everyone, regardless of their language education background. Whether you are a beginner or an advanced learner, the index is a valuable resource that will help you find the information you need efficiently.

Language education is a diverse niche, encompassing learners of various ages, cultural backgrounds, and language goals. The index of this book reflects this diversity, providing a wide range of topics that cater to the specific needs and interests of each individual. From basic phonetic principles to more advanced techniques for mastering specific sounds, the index ensures that learners can easily find the information most relevant to their pronunciation journey.

The index is not merely a list of chapter titles and page numbers. It is a carefully curated guide that offers an overview of each section, highlighting key concepts and exercises. This allows learners to get a glimpse of the content before diving into a particular chapter, enabling them to make informed choices about which topics to explore further.

Moreover, the index is a dynamic tool that facilitates cross-referencing between different sections of the book. By providing links to related topics, it ensures that readers can easily navigate the interconnected web of pronunciation skills, reinforcing their understanding and progress.

In conclusion, the index of "Perfecting Your Pronunciation: A Comprehensive Guide for Everyone" is an invaluable resource for language learners in the niche of language education. Whether you are a beginner or an advanced learner, the index will help you navigate the content of this book with ease and efficiency. By organizing the material in a way that caters to the needs and interests of diverse individuals, the index ensures that every reader can find the information they need to perfect their pronunciation skills.

In this comprehensive guide, "Perfecting Your Pronunciation: A Comprehensive Guide for Everyone," the importance of an index cannot be emphasized enough. As language education enthusiasts, we understand the struggles one faces while trying to master pronunciation in a foreign language. This subchapter, aptly titled "Index," aims to provide you with a valuable tool that will enhance your learning experience and help you navigate through the book effortlessly.

The index serves as a roadmap, allowing you to quickly locate specific topics, concepts, or exercises within the book. It organizes the content in a logical and user-friendly manner, making it easier for you to find the information you need when you need it. Whether you are a beginner or an advanced learner, this index will be your trusty companion, saving you time and effort.

Within this subchapter, you will find an alphabetical listing of all the major topics covered in "Perfecting Your Pronunciation: A Comprehensive Guide for Everyone." Each entry will include the corresponding page numbers, enabling you to jump directly to the sections that interest you the most. From basic phonetics to advanced phonological rules, from vowel sounds to consonant clusters, the index covers it all.

Furthermore, this index also includes cross-references, allowing you to explore related topics and delve deeper into specific areas of interest. For example, if you are struggling with the pronunciation of a particular sound, the index will guide you to related exercises, tips, and techniques that can help you overcome that specific challenge.

By utilizing this index effectively, you will be able to create a personalized study plan, focusing on the areas you find most challenging or intriguing. It will help you track your progress, allowing you to revisit previously studied topics and measure your improvement over time.

In conclusion, the index is an invaluable tool for all language education enthusiasts using "Perfecting Your Pronunciation: A Comprehensive Guide for Everyone." It empowers you to take control of your learning journey, making it more efficient and enjoyable. Embrace the power of the index and unlock the full potential of your pronunciation skills.